Let's Take a Leek

Let's Take a Leek

A book about a Chef, fabulous *Soups*, and a slightly different sense of humor!

Michael J. Longo, CEC

authorHOUSE®

AuthorHouse™
1663 Liberty Drive
Bloomington, IN 47403
www.authorhouse.com
Phone: 1-800-839-8640

First published by AuthorHouse   09/15/2011

ISBN: 978-1-4634-3672-8 (sc)
ISBN: 978-1-4634-4201-9 (ebk)

Library of Congress Control Number: 2011912694

Printed in the United States of America

Any people depicted in stock imagery provided by Thinkstock are models, and such images are being used for illustrative purposes only.
Certain stock imagery © Thinkstock.

This book is printed on acid-free paper.

Dedication

Dedicated to the people past, present and future who have significantly contributed to my culinary lifestyle spanning four decades. These men and women were open and willing to spend time teaching me the finer elements of the art and science of culinary preparation.

To my Mother and Grandmother (Little Nana) for patiently teaching me how to cook the old country recipes.

Most humble thanks to my Lord and Savior for allowing me to not settle for mediocrity in a life of serving Him as well as others.

Most affectionately to my wife Pam of 29 years and still counting. Pam has held the keys to my confidence and always seems to know how to build me up when I am down and remind me who I am. Thank you to my best friend, lover, cheerleader, and passionate love of my life.
Yo ti Amo

CONTENTS

Acknowledgments

In case you were wondering why I would title a cookbook called "Let's Take a Leek," I first need to take you back to a conversation I had with a co-worker. One day as we were peeling 100 pounds of onions for French Onion Soup and all the sudden he said, "Hey, why don't you write a cookbook about soups and call it . . ." Well, that's how it got started. I have compiled somewhere in the range of 130-150 soups over my career as a chef that I feel are really worth sharing. I have whittled down the number to about 55-plus Consommés and Stocks that have some great flavor profiles and nuances I'm certain you will enjoy. I will also give kudos to a number of people whom I feel have been most influential in bringing this project together. Specifically, my deepest thanks to Carol and Bill Wright, Peter Mayberry, and Annie Walters. So friends, from the hottom of my beart I really appreciate your efforts, sacrifice, and the impact you all have had on my life. May Almighty God continue to meet your every need as you touch lives wherever He leads you!

The recipes in this book do not all contain Leeks and I need to give credit to the hundreds of veggies and fruits, meats, spirits, and seasonings that combine to make these wonderful, flavorful, remarkable, and savory soups. Take this book, read it, use it to understand the method to my madness, pass on the recipes to others, and/or modify them to your own tastes. As King Solomon said in the Bible, "There is nothing new under the sun." These formulations were first practiced by Chinese cooks millenniums ago. This is intended to be a practical guide. I have scaled the recipes to yield a soup to serve 6-8 guests depending on the serving size.

My journey as an aspiring Chef has taken many years of hard work. I started in the Hotel system in 1980 when most of the cooks and chefs at the time were not willing to share a breath of air with me if there was one breath left to breathe. There was this underlying fear that the new blood might steal away their job. To the contrary, I just wanted to learn everything I could and eventually I succeeded. So, I write this to share the contents; not to simply covet the recipes and take them to the grave.

I have always believed that cooking is an emotion. It is neither masculine nor feminine. So take what ever passion you possess and use the recipes, which just might stir your culinary "pot," to make better tasting stocks and soups for you, your family, and your friends. I wish you "great taste success."

Introduction

I would say with much confidence that Webster is and was correct when he described soup as a nourishing broth containing some protein and some form of vegetables, highly seasoned, and presented as a first course or meal. As far back as biblical times we read of several accounts where a soup or a stew was involved in a very integral part of Bible history. The story of Esau and Jacob revolves around which son of Isaac would receive the blessing of his father first and thus lay claim to the eternal blessing of God Almighty. Inevitably, Jacob offered Esau a stew of lentils only if he would sell his birthright, which he did since he claimed he was starving.

As a child growing up in Iowa, I was intrigued with the woods which lay just yards from our back door in Cedar Rapids. There in the woods with my friends Jeff and Kelly, and of course our little brothers trailing behind us, we would search for food. I wanted to live off the "fat of the land." We would spend hours foraging for Morel mushrooms, pick a variety of nuts such as Black Walnuts, Hickory Nuts, and Gooseberries, but our favorite activity was to go down to Charlie's Creek. Now, I'm not sure why we called it Charlie's Creek, but what thrived in the creek were Crawdads. We would use an old fishing net to seine the flowing waters of the creek. We loved to gather them by the dozens because we knew that we could boil these beauties, peel the tails, then dip them in melted butter and eat them along with our own version of fried Morel mushrooms. The Morels were simply washed and split length-wise, dipped in egg batter, rolled in cracker crumbs, and sautéed in butter until they were golden brown and cooked through. We thought we were something back in those wooded stomping grounds. Hey, we still played football, flew kites, sandlot baseball, rode bikes, and stuff that most kids growing up in the 60's and 70's did. But, we really liked cooking any thing we could when the chance came along. I lost touch with these guys when my family and I moved to Colorado, but, I would still like to think that on occasion, those two men and perhaps their families still find themselves poking around the backwoods of Iowa searching for hidden food treasures as we did as kids.

BISQUES

Curried Tomato

When I want to make a statement about soups this is my "go to" soup. The flavor of the Tomatoes and the Curry Powder from Madras make for a great combination. What really sends this soup over the top is the Gorgonzola Crouton. If you're ready to take your favorite Tomato Soup to the next level this is the recipe for you baby! Just make sure to have extra Croutons for your family and guests. They will thank you repeatedly as they clamor for more. I can recall when I was a kid watching many a home-cook prepare a Tomato Soup from of all things a can; and adding Milk to the soup to then watch it curdle. Then guess what? The soup was served anyway, argh! This recipe will include a method to stabilize the Tomato product so the Heavy Cream can be added without the chance of it curdling.

- Let's start with what I call a Curry Reduction: Sauté Onions, Leeks, Garlic, Shallots and Curry Powder in some Butter on medium heat.
- Allow the Curry Powder to *"Bloom" and the vegetables to soften about 5 minutes.
- Add some good White Wine, lower the heat to a simmer and reduce the mixture by 1/3 of its volume.
- In a stock pot pour Tomato Puree, *Tomato Juice Cocktail and *Golden Chicken Stock together and bring the liquids to a slow boil.
- Once the Curry reduction is complete it can simply be added to the stock pot.
- Allow for the Stock, Curry reduction and Tomato products to cook for 20-30 min.
- Thicken the soup with some Cornstarch and Stock to desired viscosity and cook for 5-7 minutes to stabilize the Tomato Soup before adding the Heavy Cream. I like to heat up the Cream before adding it to the soup which helps prevent the curdling.
- Season the soup with Salt, White Pepper, Lea and Perrins, Chicken Paste and Honey Powder.
- Cook for 5 minutes more.
- Adjust seasoning to taste.
- Strain the soup through a fine mesh strainer into another soup container and keep hot for service.
- Ladle soup into bowls and float a Gorgonzola Crouton on top.
- Serve immediately.

Serves 6-8

Curry Reduction:

1 T	Madras Curry Powder
1/2 cups	Leeks (sliced)
1/2 cups	Onions (sliced)

I tsp	Fresh Garlic (crushed)
I T	Shallots (minced)
2 cups	White Wine
2 T	Butter

Soup Structure:

I -8oz. can	Tomato Puree
2 cups	V-8 Juice
I qt	*Golden Chicken Stock
2 cups	Heavy Cream
To taste	Lea and Perrins Sauce
To taste	Honey Powder
To taste	Kosher Salt
To taste	Ground White Pepper
2 T each	Cornstarch and Cold Stock

* Golden Chicken Stock: Recipe can be found in our "Take Stock" section on page 136.

Gorgonzola Croutons

1/2 cup Gorgonzola Cheese crumbled
1/2 cup soft Butter
1 French Baguette

- Mix together the Cheese and the Butter in a bowl and spread over Baguette slices.
- Broil or bake until the Cheese is melted. Serve along with the soup.

* Bloom: Culinary term to allow the herbs or spices to intensify in flavor.

* Tomato Juice Cocktail: Such as V-8.

Dilled Salmon

I love living in Colorado because the seasons are so different. If you enjoy the outdoors this is the state for you to live, love, and play in. My passion in life is any kind of fish catching. I am most passionate when it comes to fly-fishing because for me it is a contemplative type of sport. Although I thoroughly enjoy it, it has never been about catching large numbers of fish. My greatest joy is teaching a friend how to cast, drift, and hook that first fish; besides fooling a rainbow trout with an artificial fly that I hand-tied the evening before. The Kokanee Salmon or Land-locked Salmon that we are blessed to have swim in the state waters are elusive; but can be enticed with the right presentation. These fish are great fighters once they are hooked and are sometimes hard to hold on to. The average size of the Kokanee is usually between 10 and 16 inches. I have also caught a number of Kokanee through the ice during our mild winters. The brilliant orange-crimson flesh is sweet and clean largely due to the mountain spring waters, abundant aquatic food supply and fresh mountain air.

Another great way to add a flavor profile to the soup is to brine and smoke the Fish. Smokers and the instructions on "how to" are included in most of the personal smoker kits sold in those outdoor-type stores. Either way, this is a great soup to share at your next big food night.

- In a stock pot sauté Leeks, Shallots, Dill and Salmon fillets in Butter until Leeks are soft.
- Remove the cooked Salmon pieces which will be returned to the soup later in the preparation.
- Add an equal amount of Flour to absorb the butter and make a *Roux.
- Cook this on medium heat stirring until the Roux appears to take on a slightly golden-blonde color.
- Introduce *Salmon Stock, White Wine, Mace, Allspice, Dill weed, and Tomato Puree
- Allow the contents of the pot to reach a *Slow boil.
- Cook for 20-30 minutes.
- Pour Heavy Cream down the sides of the pot to minimize temperature plunge.
- Heat the soup to a slow boil and season with Salt and White Pepper.
- Place the *Cooked Salmon back into the soup and cook for 5 minutes more.
- Adjust seasoning.
- Remove the soup from the stovetop and strain the soup through a fine sieve, press the soup through the strainer with the back of a ladle or spoon into another soup pot and keep hot until service.
- Ladle soup into cups or bowls which contain some of the reserved cooked Salmon pieces, garnish with Dill Crème Fraiche. (Found at specialty food stores)

Serves 6-8

I cup	Leeks (sliced)
I cup	Onions (sliced)
I T	Shallots (minced)
3 T	Baby Dill (fresh-chopped)
4 T	Butter
4 T	Flour-all purpose
1/4 c	Tomato Puree
3-3/4 qt	Salmon Stock
I cup	White Wine
I cup	Heavy Cream
To taste	Ground Mace
To taste	Ground Allspice
To taste	Kosher Salt
To taste	Ground White Pepper

* Be sure to reserve some of the Salmon pieces for garnish or steam a fillet separately with a Dill-oil infusion for garnish only.

* Salmon Stock: Recipe can be found in our "Take Stock" section on page 135.

* Roux: Equal amounts of melted Butter and Flour cooked together to form a thickening agent for soups and stocks.

* Slow-boil: Culinary term for small bubbles just breaking the surface of the pot.

* Dill-oil infusion: Fresh or dried Dill steeped in warm oil for 10 minutes and removed from heat and allowed to cool for future preparation.

* Temperature-plunge: Occurs when a cold liquid is poured into a hot liquid slowing the cooking process.

Maine Lobster

In a small café overlooking the Inner Harbor in Baltimore, I had ordered Crab Bisque but the waitress had made a mistake on the ticket and I was pleasantly surprised with this wonderful Lobster Bisque, which was fantabulistic! The velvety smooth soup was laced with some Cognac and pieces of tender Lobster meat. I can remember my first experience with Lobster as I worked as a pantry cook at a Country Club. My numerous duties included preparing Lobster for a cold appetizer, which the members just loved. I would gently poach the treasure in some seasoned water and quickly shock them in iced-water. As I removed the meat from the shells the saucier would quickly snatch them up for a stock he was preparing for another dish. The cold Lobster meat was sliced and served over some mixed greens and garnished with Sesame Vinaigrette. I later learned from our saucier his Lobster stock recipe which is the base for this great soup, (or "stew" as labeled by some of my friends from Nova Scotia.) Anyway, looking at the massive U.S.S. Constellation sitting proudly below my perch with my soup, I suddenly found myself feeling patriotic. It would not be uncommon some 300 years ago to picture the Captain of this mighty ship being served this "rustic" recipe at his table. Perhaps it may have been served as a main dish rather than a first course, but either way I'm certain you will find it to be one of your favorites.

- Start this soup in a stock pot with some Butter to sauté some Leeks, and Celery.
- Cook on medium heat until vegetables are tender.
- Sprinkle some Flour to absorb the Butter to form a *Roux and cook, stirring to achieve a blonde color.
- Introduce the *Lobster Stock and whisk to incorporate the Roux-stock mixture.
- Add paprika, Heavy Cream, Evaporated Milk, and Whole Milk to the pot.
- Toss in the claw meat and bring all the contents of the pot to a *Slow boil.
- Allow soup to cook for 10-15 minutes to develop the flavors and the creaminess.
- Season with Sea Salt, Honey Powder and White Pepper.
- Reduce the heat to a simmer for 10 minutes.
- Remove from heat.
- Press the soup through a fine mesh strainer into a serving container and keep warm until service.
- Take the butter-poached Lobster meat which has been diced and quickly toss it in a sauté pan and *Flambé with some Cognac.
- Divide the pieces into individual bowls and pour the hot soup over the pieces and serve immediately.

Serves 6-8

* Butter-poaching: Culinary term for gently cooking seafood in a mixture of 2/3 whole butter to 1/3 water until it is fully cooked.

* Butter-poaching the lobster meat is a great method to cook the lobster which will keep it delicate and tender for the final garnishment.

BUTTER-POACHING METHOD FOR LOBSTER

1	Maine Lobster 1-1/2 to 2 lb. (live)
	Dispatch the Lobster with a sharp knife through the top of the head
	Split length-wise and carefully remove meat from tail and claws reserve
	for butter-stock; use shells, claws and legs for *Lobster stock.
2 cups	Whole butter
4 cups	Water

SOUP STRUCTURE

1/2 cup	Leeks (sliced)
1/2 cup	Celery (sliced)
4 T	Butter
4 T	Flour-all purpose
1 qt	*Lobster Stock
2 T	Spanish Paprika
1 cup	Heavy Cream
1 cup	Evaporated Milk
1 cup	Whole Milk
To taste	Sea Salt
To taste	White Pepper
To taste	Honey Powder
2 oz.	Cognac

* Slow boil: Culinary term for small bubbles just breaking the surface of the pot.

* Lobster Stock: Recipe can be found in our "Take Stock" section on page 134.

* Roux: Equal amounts of melted butter and flour cooked together to form a thickening agent for soups and stocks.

* Flambe: To cook using an alcohol-based liquid to quickly flavor (ignite the alcohol) or finish a dish.

Mushroom and Clam

This soup is where land and sea meet to form a great relationship of flavors. I first learned how to make this soup working in one of Colorado Springs' finest resort hotels. Roasting the mushrooms will enhance and deepen the flavors. On the Clam side of the equation the fresher the Clams the better. If not available those of us in the Midwest will look for the best canned or frozen Clams we can purchase. The Clams were packaged in a plastic netted bag, and the Mushrooms were in small boxes of differing varieties. This is where the real work began of soup making. My apprentice and I would steam the Clams, cool them down, and then start pulling the meat out of the shells. We would need enough Clams for 30 gallons of soup. Keep in mind we changed the soup daily so this was one soup that we made about every 9 weeks. As a rule we would try to work a day ahead of ourselves to keep pace with the rest of the production schedule. This method would allow us to quickly put a soup together without having to spend time still preparing Clams or roasting the Mushrooms. The Mushrooms would be several varieties from Chanterelles, Shitake, Wood Ear, Morel, etc. These would be tossed in some Butter and then placed in a 400° F. oven until they were roasted and took on a much deeper earthy flavor profile.

The following recipe will instruct you on how to prepare the soup using a *Veloute sauce which combines Clam juice and Chicken stock along with a *Roux and the addition of Heavy Cream to create the bisque-like smoothness needed for this great soup.

- In a stock pot start with some melted Butter and Flour (equal amounts).
- Cook this on medium heat to achieve a blonde appearance with a slight nuttiness.
- Quickly add the two liquids of equal parts, stirring to form a semi-thick sauce.
- Cook this mixture on medium heat *Slow boil occasionally stirring to break up any large lumps for about 20-30 minutes.
- Introduce the Heavy Cream down the sides of the pot to minimize the *Temperature plunge.
- Heat the soup contents of the pot up to a slow boil again and season with Salt, White Pepper and Lea and Perrins Sauce.
- Cook for 10 minutes more and remove from heat.
- Pour contents through a fine mesh strainer into another serving container.
- Add the cooked Clams and roasted Mushrooms to the pot, return to the stove top on medium heat to warm up the Clams and Mushrooms (5-6 minutes).
- Ladle into bowls or cups and garnish with fresh snipped Chives and serve immediately.

Serves 6-8

6 T	Butter
6 T	Flour-all purpose
1 qt	Clam juice
1 qt	*Golden Chicken Stock
2 cups	Wild Mushrooms: Chanterelles, Shitake, Wood Ear, Morels
2 cups	Heavy Cream
2 cups	Chopped Clams or 2-3 dozen Manila or Cherrystone Clams
To taste	Kosher Salt
To taste	Ground White Pepper
To taste	Lea and Perrins Sauce
2 T	Fresh Chives (snipped)

- Steam the clams in a pot with some good beer until the clam shells open. Cool, shuck and store in the refrigerator until needed. (Save some time and prepare the clams a day ahead.)
- Toss cleaned, sliced mushrooms in some melted butter and roast in a 400° F oven for 30-40 minutes or longer if needed. Cool and refrigerate until needed.

* Golden Chicken Stock: Recipe can be found in our "Take Stock" section on page 136.

* Veloute sauce: Mother sauce used as a base to create soups and sauces.

* Slow boil: Culinary term for small bubbles just breaking the surface of the pot.

* Temperature plunge: Occurs when a cold liquid is introduced into a hot liquid which slows the cooking process.

* Roux: Equal amounts of melted butter and flour cooked together to form a thickening agent for soups and stocks.

CHILLED SOUPS

Banana Soup

Ooh Walla Ooh Walla Banana! I don't know what it means other than once you taste this great soup you may start your own banana-themed chant. A myriad of flavors will pass over your palate with each spoonful so hang on or hang ten. Ripe Bananas are certainly the key to this soup's success. (Save the overripe ones with lots of sugar spots for that banana bread or muffin thing.) I used to make this recipe for the boys and I would let them help me. This is a good way to teach our children about different methods of food production as well; I believe it is very important as adults to not allow our personal food prejudices' to shape the way our children eat. With their tiny palates in the developmental stage I would allow the boys to taste everything and anything just to learn the different flavors. This would allow them to form their own opinion as to what foods they liked and disliked. This is a quick recipe to make so please be sure the blender top is fastened tightly before hitting the puree button or the fun will change quickly to a cleaning chore. Okay, moms and dads please feel free to omit the rum for the children's sake.

- In a blender or food processor place Bananas, Coconut Milk, Sour Cream, Vanilla Extract, and Heavy Cream.
- Pulse gently to incorporate all ingredients then let her rip to a smooth consistency.
- Add a touch of Honey to sweeten the soup if needed.
- Chill until service.
- Stir into the soup 2-3 oz. Jamaican Rum. Just for kicks and giggles serve the soup in chilled bowls or cups garnished with fresh diced pineapple, shredded coconut, and sliced bananas.

Serves 6-8

6 each	Ripe Bananas (large and peeled)
2 cups	Coconut Milk
2 cups	Sour Cream
2 cups	Pineapple juice
2 T	Vanilla extract
2 T	Honey
2-3 oz.	Dark Rum

Cucumber Soup

As a matter of fact the Cucumber is the coolest vegetable in the garden. The Cucumber can be as much as 10 degrees cooler according to some scientific-type dudes. Nana would describe for me the way she and her sisters would eat Cucumber sandwiches when there was nothing else to eat. She would take Bread and spread Butter over the two slices, add sliced Cucumbers fresh from the field and season with Salt and Pepper. This is the reason I have always promoted the use of local produce when available. It is within my heritage to grow and harvest from the ground as my family has done for decades. When available I will always use products from the Farmer's Market. The best part of the equation is that I still know the farmers on the St. Charles Mesa east of Pueblo. If you are not able to source the local produce, the English or European type cucumbers will work as well.

This soup is very straight forward in the preparation. This makes for easy work in the kitchen when preparing for that summer garden party with family and friends. I like to serve this soup as an appetizer.

- Using a blender or food processor, puree the seeded Cucumbers and fresh Baby Dill.
- Lightly season the puree with Salt and White Pepper.
- Refrigerate this mix overnight. Remove from the refrigerator and add Heavy Cream to reach desired consistency and mouth-feel.
- Adjust seasoning as needed and serve chilled with a dollop of Crème Fraiche and a tiny sprinkle of fresh Baby Dill.

Serves 6-8

12-14 each	Cucumbers-medium (peeled, seeded and sliced)
3 T	Fresh Baby Dill
3-4 cups	Heavy Cream
To taste	Kosher Salt
To taste	Ground White Pepper
4-6 oz.	*Crème Fraiche

* Crème Fraiche: Can be purchased at most food specialty stores.

Colorado Gazpacho

I have read of a few different explanations as to the origin of Gazpacho. The Andalusian region of Southern Spain is said to be the birthplace, and I would agree with that, as I have been the recipient of many dishes created by my fellow colleagues through the network of our prestigious occupation, who pride themselves in their wonderful Spanish heritage. By all means though, give me the real deal. I don't want White Gazpacho, nor do I want Watermelon Gazpacho. I want the "Big Red". This is the starter for those garden parties in Martha's Vineyard or LaJolla Beach dinners.

- In a blender or food processor start with Cucumbers, Tomatoes, fresh Garlic, dried bread, roasted Almonds, and red Pimientos.
- Add about 1/2 of the Tomato Juice, which will help to puree the solids.
- When the mix looks like a rainbow of colors, add the Olive Oil, seasonings, and remainder of the Tomato Juice.
- Adjust to taste using the Vinegar, Honey Powder, Salt and White Pepper.
- If the consistency of the soup is still too thick, add some cold Beef consommé. This will boost the flavors, but won't compete with the Tomatoes.
- Chill until service.
- Serve the soup in chilled bowls or cups.
- Garnish with diced Cucumber, sliced Scallions, diced Avocado, or my favorite cooked and peeled Gulf Shrimp. Let the fiesta begin.

Serves 6-8

8 each	Cucumbers (peeled, seeded and sliced)
12 each	Tomatoes (peeled and diced)
1/2 cup	Red Pimientos
1/2 cup	Roasted Almonds
2 slices	Bread (dried)
64 oz.	Tomato Juice
2 cups	Beef consommé
2 T	Fresh Garlic (crushed)
2 T	Cumin Powder
1/4 cup	Olive Oil
1/4 cup	Red Wine Vinegar
To taste	Honey Powder
To taste	Kosher Salt
To taste	Ground White Pepper

Melon Soup

This is one of those versatile soup recipes where anything goes, so don't be bashful with your own sense of creativity. I can remember a few years ago while working for the Kissing Camel's Golf Club; I had to scold the bartender for mistaking my Melon soup for his froo-froo drink mix. Somehow it was "mismarked" he said. Well, I can't blame him. Marked or not it was an easy chore to make up another batch.

This is a very straight forward recipe to make so be sure to remove all the undesirable seeds and pithy white or green from the Melons you choose. I like to start with a base for these fruit soups and the choices are endless. I like to use a little simple syrup but fruit juices are good as long as they don't dominate the flavor profile. Choose either simple syrup or a juice base such as Apple or Pineapple.

- Place the syrup and peeled, seeded Melons in the blender or food processor and blend until smooth and velvety. I like to use a combination of Cantaloupe, Honeydew, Musk or Watermelon.
- Check soup for the right mouth-feel, consistency and flavor. Adjust accordingly.
- Pour in 2-3 oz. of Jamaican Rum.
- Serve in chilled cups garnished with some *Candied Fruit Nibs. Maybe even a crazy straw for fun.

Serves 6-8

*CANDIED FRUIT NIBS

This is the Candied Fruit recipe you always wanted to learn.

- Simply take the peel from 1 Orange, Lemon, and Lime.
- Trim away a good bit of the pithy white stuff and dice the colored peel finely.
- Place the diced Fruit peels in a solution of 2 parts granulated Sugar to 1 part water and heat to a boil.
- Reduce heat to simmer and cook until the mixture is nearly the consistency of syrup.
- Strain the fruit from the syrup and pour onto waxed paper and sprinkle again with granulated Sugar allow to dry overnight.
- Break up pieces into tiny "nibs."

2 qt	Simple syrup (2 parts water to 1 part granulated Sugar over low heat until dissolved. Chill before using) or juice base.
1 each	Cantaloupe, Honeydew and 1/4 of a Watermelon (peeled and seeded.)
2-3 oz.	Jamaican Rum

Strawberry Soup

Let's celebrate the Strawberry shall we? From bad press in the 1900's to the number one position of today, this baby berry has come a long way! Once considered to be poisonous of all things, I have had this berry in everything from appetizer to dessert. This recipe starts with a little simple syrup, fresh Mint and Basil.

- Prepare the simple syrup by mixing 2 parts water to 1 part granulated Sugar in a sauce pot on low heat.
- Introduce chopped fresh Mint and Basil leaves in equal amounts. Do not boil just let this steep once the Sugar is dissolved.
- Remove from heat and place the mix into a gallon sized container.
- Here comes the FUN part, Add fresh sliced Strawberries to the mix and refrigerate overnight.

- Once chilled, remove from the refrigerator or cooler and into a blender.
- Add Heavy Cream in small amounts as the soup blends together on a low speed.
- Keep adding the Cream as needed and taste to desired flavor and consistency.
- Strain to remove the hulls through a very fine mesh strainer.

Now, for a great milkshake for the kids:

- Add Vanilla Ice Cream and omit the rum.

And for the adults, who would rather have the soup for dessert

- Be liberal with the Rum and Ice Cream.
- Return to the refrigerator to chill until service.
- Remove from refrigerator and add 2-3 oz. of Jamaican Rum.
- Ladle into chilled bowls and garnish with fresh diced Strawberries.
- Serve it with a smile!

Serves 6-8

2 qt	Simple syrup (2 parts water to 1 part sugar)
2 pints	Fresh Strawberries (hulled and sliced)
1 oz	Fresh Basil leaves
1 oz	Fresh Mint
1-2 pints	Heavy Cream
2-3 oz	Jamaican Rum
1 pint	Fresh Strawberries (diced bite-size for garnish)

Vichyssoise

If you love potatoes, this is one soup for those warm summer nights. Don't mention this to the French but this could be heated and served hot. I wouldn't though, it would be just as they say, "C'est ridicule nes pa" (That's ridiculous.)

Choose a good potato to make the base for the soup. Look for Russets or even Yukon Gold for a couple of choices.

- I like to start with Leeks, Onions and Celery in a rough chop since we will be pureeing the finished product.
- Give this a quick sauté with a little Butter until tender.
- Introduce *Golden Chicken Stock, Bay Leaf and peeled, rough-cut potatoes.
- Bring the contents of the pot up to a slow boil, reduce heat and cook until the potatoes are fork tender and stock is reduced.
- Remove the Bay leaf before pureeing the soup.
- Season with Salt, White Pepper, and Chicken Paste to boost flavors.
- Cool in the refrigerator over night covered.
- When completely chilled, taste the soup for seasoning.
- Add Heavy Cream to the soup to give it the proper *Viscosity and mouth feel.
- Taste for seasoning, adjust if needed and chill until service.
- Serve in chilled bowls and garnish the soup with fresh snipped Chives.

Serves 6-8

I cup	Leeks (white part only, chopped)
I cup	Onions (chopped)
I cup	Celery (chopped)
4 T	Butter
2 lb	Potatoes (peeled and chopped)
3 qt	*Golden Chicken Stock
2 each	Bay Leaf
I-2 pints	Heavy Cream
To taste	Chicken paste
To taste	Ground White Pepper
To taste	Kosher Salt
I oz	Fresh snipped Chives

* Golden Chicken Stock: Recipe can be found in our "Take Stock" section on page 136.

* Viscosity: Thickness of how a soup appears.

CHOWDERS

Boston Clam

Let's do away with semantics. We'll call it Boston, since Pam and I were traveling the New England states one fine autumn day and reluctantly stumbled into this little seafood restaurant to ask for directions to my nephew Shree's house. As the hostess was trying to show me where I was and where I needed to be on one of those silly tourist type maps, you know the ones that aren't really to scale and by the time you realize it, you don't want to go back and shake their throat in thanks for giving you directions that confuse you more because now you're really lost and running short of time. Needless to say, we were only a 1/2 hour late largely not to my poor sense of direction, but because the take-out line in the restaurant was long. Let me explain, while I was talking to the hostess about directions I spotted this bowl of creamy, clammy goodness. So naturally, being a chef I had to order two quarts to take to my nephew as a housewarming gift. Let me tell you this was the reason to come to Boston, (sorry Shree and Jodi, I love you and your family but you're a real close second.) Once the hugs and kisses were over and blessings given; we quickly assembled our plates. This chowder was a big hit way out of the park. Frankly, the chowder was very basic in structure. The lynch-pin was the fresh Clams that were first steamed in some local ale and then chopped and tossed into the velvety white sauce.

- Let's begin this journey toward chowder-land with a stock pot to which we have rendered some good smoky Bacon.
- Add in some additional Oil or Butter and pour in the vegetables.
- Sauté the vegetables in the pot with the Bacon for 5 minutes until the vegetables are partially cooked.
- Sprinkle in some fresh Thyme leaves followed by an amount of Flour equal to fat.
- Stir to form a *Roux with the vegetables intertwined with the fat and Flour.
- Cook and stir until the Roux takes on a blonde appearance (about 4-6 minutes.)
- Pour *Fish Stock and Clam juice into the pot and stir to mix completely.
- Allow the contents of the pot to reach a *Slow boil and cook for 20-25 minutes, stirring occasionally.
- At this point introduce the Heavy Cream along the sides of the pot to minimize the *Temperature plunge. This will allow the soup to resume the original boil in a quicker time.
- Add the *Par-cooked Potatoes and season with Clam paste, White Pepper, and Lea and Perrins Sauce.
- Cook until the Potatoes are tender (8-10 minutes.)
- Thicken if needed with Cornstarch and Clam juice and continue to cook for 5 minutes more.
- Adjust seasoning to taste and bring on the chopped Clams right into the pot.

- Remove from heat and ladle into Sourdough Bread bowls and garnish with Oyster Crackers and fresh chopped Parsley.
- Serve immediately.

Serves 6-8

1/2 lb	Bacon (Hickory smoked and diced)
1 cup	Leeks (diced)
1 cup	Onions (diced)
1 cup	Celery (diced)
1 cup	Green Peppers (diced)
8 oz	Melted Butter or Oil
8 oz	Flour-all purpose
2 T	Thyme Leaves (fresh)
1 qt	Clam Juice
1 qt	*Fish Stock
1 pint	Heavy Cream
2 lb	Potatoes (peeled, diced and par-cooked)
To taste	Clam Paste
To taste	Sea Salt
To taste	Ground White Pepper
To taste	Lea and Perrins Sauce
2-4 T each	Cornstarch and Cold Stock mixed together
2 T	Parsley (chopped)

* Fish Stock: Recipe can be found in our "Take Stock" section on page 133.

* Par-cooked: Culinary term used to partially cook a food product (e.g. boil the diced potatoes for the Chowder in some salted water until the potatoes are cooked 50%.)

* Temperature plunge: Occurs when a cold liquid is introduced into a hot liquid slowing the cooking process.

* Roux: Equal parts of melted butter and flour cooked together and used as a thickening agent for soups and stocks.

* Slow boil: Culinary term for bubbles just breaking the surface of the pot.

Cajun Oyster

Oysters! Oysters! Raw! Raw! Raw! Aw shucks! What else can I say about this great soup? A cook worth his keep needs to learn all he or she can about how to prepare a myriad of food products. The wealth of knowledge one possesses is generally equal to the number of life experiences about a specific subject they have learned; namely culinary arts. My experience with shucking Clams and Oysters goes back to my days at the Pueblo Country Club. This is where the "talk of the town" got its start. I was a pantry cook at that time when the C.F. & I. Steel Mill was booming and the golf course bar was full of stuffed shirts playing the old one-upmanship game. I didn't have time to eavesdrop on the conversation as the bartenders' helper did; I was learning things about food I never new existed. The chef was a Culinary Institute Grad and had a Santa-type appearance and demeanor. He was always willing to teach when time permitted and I did learn many techniques from his tutelage. He was from New England so when it came to anything, be it Mollusks, Crustaceans, and Fish, Chef John had the knowledge to demonstrate the methods of preparation of each prize from the oceans' blue. So when he came to me with a barrel of Oysters that were in need of shucking; I was, shall we say, over eager to learn. So with knife and towel in hand I began the "how" to prying open each shell. Shucking Oysters also gave me the opportunity to learn how to eat these gems of the sea. It wasn't long after that I was teaching others "how to" on the Oysters. The best time I can remember with Oysters was a time about 2 years later still working for Chef John; he asked me to oversee the Sunday Brunch for the members. I instructed the pantry staff to set-up the Seafood display and to take turns hand-shucking the Oysters as guests strolled through the buffet line. The fun came into play when two of the pantry staff reported to work "hung-over" from the night before. Can you smell the rubber burning and hear the wheels turning? These two unfortunate souls were chosen by "yours truly" to attend the Oyster bar for the duration of the brunch. The first recipient shucked 2 Oysters before she literally turned green in front of all of us, including the guests. The second person only needed to smell the Oyster bar before abruptly leaving the station to find the facilities. It was a good laugh and a lesson to the two workers who pleaded with me to do anything but shuck Oysters again.

All jokes aside, this is a great recipe for those of us who love Oysters sober or not.

- Start with a sauté of Onion, Celery, diced Potatoes, and some chopped Garlic in a stock pot.
- Cook for 6-8 minutes—stir to keep the Garlic from browning too quickly.
- Introduce some *Fish Stock and White Wine to the vegetables and bring the contents of the pot to a mild simmer.
- Cook for 30-40 minutes, mildly simmering to allow the flavors to develop fully.

- Season the soup with Light Soy Sauce, Louisiana Hot Pepper Sauce and White Pepper.
- Add the raw Oysters and let the whole pot cook for another 10 minutes or until the Oysters are heated through.
- Remove from the heat and ladle into bowls, serve with good Bread.

Serves 6-8

1 cup	Celery (diced)
1 cup	Onions (diced)
2 lb	Potatoes (peeled and diced in ½ inch cubes)
2 T	Fresh Garlic (chopped)
2 qt	*Fish Stock
2 cups	White Wine
To taste	Light Soy Sauce
To taste	Louisiana Hot Pepper Sauce
To taste	Ground White Pepper
1 qt	Fresh shucked Oysters or about 2-1/2 dozen shucked with liquor

* Fish Stock: Recipe can be found in our "Take Stock" section on page 133.

Conch

On a trip to San Diego years ago, as my bride and I walked barefoot on the beach, we stopped to collect the prettiest shells we could find. However, we did not find a Conch shell but we found a great bowl of chowder at this highly publicized seaside restaurant. As most people would say, "You had to have been there" to appreciate the mélange of flavors and textures which comprised this soup. I had worked with Conch once before, but somehow it was not the same. I would get that response from guests in my restaurant as they would explain to me that they just came back from a trip to Italy and wanted to recreate the experience. I'd simply reply, there are three things in this world we cannot duplicate—friends, songs, and recipes. There is so much emotion that we exert in the people we love, the music we create, and the foods we eat. As cooks and chefs we do our best to practice cooking consistently with the food offerings we prepare for our patrons. This is why they keep coming back and hopefully back again. The great philosopher Willy Wonka used to say, "We are the music makers and we are the dreamers of dreams." In the kitchen we are the champions of the monotonous and mundane. But, we keep doing what we do because we like the end result. We create and re-create to keep the cycle going. I've often heard in my own kitchens the "under the breath" complaints of too many "tickets." As a business owner I want to hear that everyday, but not to the point of frustration to my cooks. And that's where the training comes in to play. Keeping things fresh! That is it! It was the freshness of the Conch that made the dish in San Diego taste so much better. When I look into my minds eye I can't just see the ocean, I can smell it and feel it. I can hear it as well. That is why we carefully write down recipes and keep them from being lost or misplaced. By consistent execution of cooking techniques and principles we serve great tasting food each and everyday that we hang out the "open" sign.

- In a stock pot sauté Bacon, Carrots, Celery, Leeks, Green Peppers, Onion and Potatoes until the Onions are translucent.
- Sprinkle in the seasonings along with some *Fish stock, diced Tomatoes, Tomato juice and bring the contents of the pot to a slow boil.
- Reduce heat to a simmer add the Conch meat and simmer for 30-35 minutes.
- Season the soup with Clam paste, Hot Pepper Sauce and White Pepper.
- Cook 5 minutes more, remove from heat, ladle into bowls or cups and serve immediately.

Serves 6-8

1/2 lb	Hickory smoked Bacon (diced)
1 cup	Carrot (diced)
1 cup	Celery (diced)
1 cup	Green peppers (diced)

1 cup	Leeks (sliced-white part only)
1 cup	Onion (diced)
2 lb	Potatoes (peeled and diced)
4 T	Butter
2 T	Fresh Garlic
2 T	Thyme Leaves
2 each	Bay Leaves
2 cups	Tomato Juice
1 cup	Tomatoes (diced)
2 qt	*Fish Stock
1-1/2 lb	Fresh or frozen Conch meat (ground)
To taste	Clam paste
To taste	Ground White Pepper
To taste	Hot Pepper Sauce

* Fish Stock: Recipe can be found in our "Take Stock" section on page 133.

Manhattan Clam

I love Manhattan! There are very few places you can take the subway and spend the day eating your way through the city. The "big apple" had a much different atmosphere from just six years earlier when I was taking my test for certification as an Executive Chef. Somehow and someway it felt safer, warmer, better. Maybe I was so focused on myself that I really didn't make the time to enjoy the sights, sounds, smells, and tastes that were all around me. We traveled to New York as a family shortly after the 9/11 disaster. It is true we wept as we peered through the fence at the devastation. People were so friendly to us when we got turned around and lost. But, today we were together as a family eating giant pretzel and slices of pizza a foot long and you had to fold them over to take a bite. I had always debated in my mind which Chowder was better, New England or Manhattan. I figured now that I am in the city that boasts about all its culture and cuisine, I needed to try it. We walked quite a ways which means quite a ways, and found a street vendor all set up to sell me the goods. Just as I suspected that first spoonful of the red stuff said it all for me. Clams, tomatoes, and potatoes along with some good seasoned broth—it was great! This gentleman we will name Saresh had other soup offerings but this is what I had set my sights on. So, I want to share the experience with all of you who thumb through the pages of this book.

- Start the soup by sautéing Celery, Green Peppers, Onions and Potatoes.
- Cook for 6-8 minutes and sprinkle in some Thyme.
- Introduce Clam Juice and Tomato Juice and allow the contents of the pot to reach a slow boil.
- Reduce the heat to a simmer and cook for 30-40 minutes.
- Pour in fresh Chopped Clams, stir, season with Sea Salt, Ground White Pepper, and clam paste.
- Continue heating the pot until it reaches a simmer.
- Thicken the soup with Cornstarch and Clam Juice and cook 5 minutes more.
- Adjust seasoning to taste, sprinkle with fresh chopped Parsley and serve with those little Oyster-type crackers.

Serves 6-8

1 cup	Celery (diced)
1 cup	Green Pepper (diced)
1 cup	Onion (diced)
2 lb	Potatoes (peeled and diced)
2 T	Fresh Thyme Leaves
1 qt	Clam Juice
1 qt	Tomato Juice

1 qt	Fresh or frozen Clams (2-3 dozen manila or cherrystone clams steamed and shucked
To taste	Clam Paste
To taste	Ground White Pepper
To taste	Sea Salt
2-4 T each	Cornstarch and Clam Juice mixed together
2 T Fresh	Parsley (chopped)

Roasted Corn and Potato

From the heartland from whence I came; this soup comes from the great state of Iowa where everything and everybody is corn-fed including this chef and darn proud of it. As much grief that I get from people who have never seen Iowa, but feel they have a right to tell me all about it from traveling Interstate 80, I respond by saying, "Take a long potty-break for about 3 days and experience the sights, sounds, humidity, and smells of this great state." Never have I seen bluer skies or greener hills and fields, as well as abundant wildlife and plant-life. A line in one of my favorite musicals about Iowa says, "You simply ought to give Iowa a try." Just for the record I have a friend who was gracious enough to give me a key to her cottage on Lake Okoboji so if you're ever in the neighborhood come by and "drown" a worm with me. By golly we might even stir-up a pot of Roasted Corn and Potato Chowder to go with some fresh grilled Walleye Fillets.

This soup is a perennial favorite of my family and I'm sure that once you have made a pot you'll agree. I want to make certain that we can all get on the fresh Corn wagon and jump off the Frozen or canned Corn wagons. The taste difference is more than just night and day, it is planetary. I have soaked roasting ears in salted water and then shucked them on the grill for an hour or more which truly are a labor of love, but cooking the ears and cutting the kernels off the cob then roasting the Butter coated pieces of gold in a 450° F. oven is much easier. To double your pleasure in this recipe we will also roast the Potatoes for twice the flavor.

- In a stock pot, heat some Butter or Oil in which the Onions and Leeks are to be sautéed.
- Cook for 6-8 minutes until the vegetables are tender and somewhat golden in appearance.
- Add the roasted Corn, *Golden Chicken Stock, Chicken Paste, fresh Ginger, and Ground White Pepper.
- Bring the contents of the pot to a slow boil and cook for 15-20 minutes.
- Pour the Heavy Cream down the sides of the pot into the soup to minimize the *Temperature plunge.
- Add the Potatoes and cook until the soup returns to a boil.
- Thicken if desired with Cornstarch and Cold Stock.
- Cook 5 minutes more adjust seasoning as needed.
- Garnish as you wish and serve immediately.

Serves 6-8

1/2 cup	Leeks (sliced)
1/2 cup	Onions (sliced)

1 lb	Fresh Corn (buttered and roasted in a 450° F oven)
1 lb	Yukon Gold Potatoes (peeled and diced 1/2 inch roasted with the corn)
2 T	Butter or Oil
4 cups	*Golden Chicken Stock
3 cups	Heavy Cream
To taste	Chicken Paste
To taste	Fresh Ginger
To taste	Ground White Pepper
To taste	Kosher Salt

* Golden Chicken Stock: Recipe can be found in our "Take Stock" section on page 136.

* Temperature plunge: Occurs when a cold liquid is introduced into a hot liquid slowing down the cooking process.

Smoked Pheasant and Corn

Once while driving through Kansas, my family and I were trying to find a famous Fried Chicken restaurant in a town called Brookings. We finally found it and had one of the best fried chicken dinners ever. You know . . . the person who invented the boneless skinless chicken breast should be tarred and feathered and sent out on a rail. How could you let that poor bird die in vain? Leave the skin on that chicken and let it be fried to a golden brown and served with mashed potatoes and a lake of gravy. I'm sure that's what the good Lord intended when He created that bird. So the families' back in the car, it is autumn, and were driving down this country road when out of the ditch beside the road flies this ring neck. Wham! He hits the wind shield and careens off toward the back of the minivan. I watch in horror through my rear-view mirror as he hit the dusty road and lay lifeless. So, as I stopped the van and put it in park, the boys were out the door before me. It was such a beautiful bird with all the colorful plumage-less a few feathers. Shortly after, these two hunter-type guys come from out of the adjacent field with their shotguns safely secured and asked me what I was going to do with the bird. I replied, "Well I'd like to cook it but, I don't have a license to take him". The men just smiled and said, "Good answer, because we are undercover for the Kansas Division of Wildlife and we wanted to see what you were going do with the bird being that your van has a Colorado license plate." One of the officers (as I now thought I should address them) asked me how I would cook the pheasant. I told them because the bird got bludgeoned with the windshield, it would be best to clean him, brine him, and smoke him in a hickory smoker for about 4-6 hours. These guys got big grins on their faces as I wrote down how to brine and smoke the bird. One officer replied, "Why so long to smoke the bird?" I said, "It takes a long time to keep the tail lit." With a chuckle the senior officer, we'll call him Jim, told us they weren't going to forget to tell everyone we know there are some nice folks that live in Colorado. I replied I would appreciate that very much. And so goes the inspiration into this wonderful bowl of goodness.

- In a stock pot sauté Celery, Leeks, Onions, diced Potatoes, and kernel Corn in a Little Butter or Oil for 4-6 minutes.
- Introduce some *Golden Chicken or *Pheasant Stock along with a *Sachet bag consisting of: 1 Bay Leaf, 1 sprig of fresh Thyme, and 1 T crushed Black Peppercorns.
- Allow this to reach a slow boil.
- Reduce heat to a simmer for 20-25 minutes or until the Potatoes are cooked through.
- Remove the Sachet bag and pour Heavy Cream down the side of the pot to reduce *Temperature plunge.
- Season soup with Chicken paste to fortify the flavor, Ground White Pepper and Salt.
- Bring the soup back to a simmer (6-8 minutes.)

- Thicken as desired with Cornstarch and some cold stock.
- Adjust seasoning to taste.
- At this point add bite-size pieces of smoked Pheasant or for that matter any smoked meat you enjoy.
- Cook long enough to reheat the Pheasant pieces and remove from stove top.
- Ladle into bowls or cups and serve immediately.

Serves 6-8

I cup	Celery (diced)
I cup	Onions (diced)
I cup	Leeks (diced, white-part only)
3 cups	Fresh Corn
3 cups	Potatoes (diced 1/2 inch cubes)
2 qt	*Pheasant Stock
1-1/2 cups	Heavy Cream
Sachet bag	Bay Leaf, fresh Thyme, Black Peppercorns (crushed)
3 cups	Smoked Pheasant meat (diced)
To taste	Chicken Paste
To taste	Ground White Pepper
To taste	Kosher Salt
2 T	Liquid Smoke flavoring
3 T each	Cornstarch and Cold Stock

* Golden Chicken Stock: Recipe can be found in our "Take Stock" section on Page 136.

* Pheasant Stock: Recipe can be found in our "Take Stock" section on page 137.

* Sachet bag: Culinary term for spices and aromatics tied up into a cheesecloth bag to enhance the flavor of a soup or stock.

* Temperature plunge: Occurs when a cold liquid is introduced into a hot liquid which slows down the cooking process.

CLASSIC

Avgolemono

If you remember the chronological order of the development of the culinary arts, the ingredient list and methodology of this soup might ring clear in your thought process. The Chinese were the first cooks in the civilized world to develop most of the dishes we eat today. I'm not speaking about how Americans eat, but worldwide our gastronomic roots have intertwined for centuries. You may not realize that the food from the Caribbean Islands have indeed, African and Asian influence. In South America, for example, over the centuries we have had German, Dutch, and Japanese influence in the cuisine. Let me explain it. Not all the food offerings in Caracas are some form of taco or enchilada. The cuisine of Antigua, Guatemala is not just corn and beans. Although, each region may share the same indigenous crops, there is a plethora of new and exciting ingredients either being grown or imported to enrich or enhance the abundant flavors with which to cook many of the foods we eat in and around the globe. This melting pot of cultures, ingredients, and methods have given birth to the foods we chefs plate up and serve to millions each day. The evolution of Avgolemono Soup is a derivation of the Egg Drop Soup developed by our fellow Chinese cooks. While working for a very passionate Greek businessman, I'll call him Gus, I learned many dishes from a wealth of knowledge this man possessed in his head. He was not a *TRAINED* cook by any standards, but in his own words, said, "I remember the flavors of the food from my Mother's kitchen and that is what I want to share with you." For 4 months we experimented with everything from grape leaves to fresh fish to recreate those flavors from his youth. I can assure you of one thing, the Greeks will use lemon and garlic on just about everything. This soup is easy to make if you follow the instructions carefully.

- Begin with a *Golden Chicken Stock in a 3-quart stock pot.
- Bring the stock up to a simmer.
- Add the long-grain Rice and cook partially covered for about 12 minutes until the Rice is tender.
- Season the broth with Salt and Ground White Pepper.
- Take a stainless steel bowl and whisk the Egg Yolks along with 2 tablespoons of fresh Lemon juice.
- Continue to whisk until the mixture is smooth and bubbly.
- Now, place the bowl on a flat surface with a kitchen towel wrapped underneath the bowl (this will keep the bowl from teetering or spinning while you whisk the hot soup into the Egg-Lemon juice mixture.)
- Add approximately 4 oz. of hot soup into the bowl and whisk as it is poured. This would be similar to the method for streaming clarified Butter into a bowl of *Tempered yolks for making Hollandaise Sauce.

- Remove the soup from heat and slowly add the Egg mixture, which you have now *Tempered, to prevent curdling the soup.
- Continue to whisk as needed.
- Adjust seasoning if needed.
- Ladle soup into cups or bowls and garnish with a slice of Lemon and chopped fresh Parsley.
- Serve immediately.

Serves 6-8

3-3/4 cups	*Golden Chicken Stock
1/3 cup	Long grain Rice
3	Egg Yolks
2	Lemons
2 T	Parsley (chopped)
To taste	Kosher Salt
To taste	White Pepper

* Golden Chicken Stock: Recipe can be found in our "Take Stock" section on page 136.

* Tempered: Culinary term for adding a small amount of hot liquid into relatively cooler egg yolks in order to warm them without scrambling.

Beef Barley Soup

Beef and Barley Dude! What a great soup to serve to guests coming in from the cold. The soup is beefy, hearty and chock full of great tasting vegetables. I ordered this soup at many a diner only to be disappointed with the presentation and contents of the bowl. Ugh! Either I can barely find the Barley or barely is there any broth because the Barley had absorbed all of it. This is a good "do ahead of time soup then put it in the crock pot and see you later." But, this is where a little forethought comes into play. If you add the cooked Barley to the soup and place it in the crock pot to simmer for hours the result will be a massive glob of Barley, vegetables, and meat with no liquid. Since the Barley is a grain it will act like pasta absorbing most of the broth. So cook the Barley and cool it down. Refrigerate it until you're ready to serve and then simply fill the bowls or cups with as much of the grain as you choose and pour the hot soup over the top of it and serve.

- In a stock pot sauté Carrots, Celery, Onions, and Turnip in a little Olive Oil until tender.
- Pour in *Rich Beef Stock and bring up to a slow boil.
- Reduce heat to a simmer and cook 20-25 minutes.
- Add diced cooked Beef and 1-2 tablespoons of Beef paste to fortify the broth.
- Cook Barley in a separate pot per instructions on package, rinse in cold water and refrigerate.
- Season the soup with *Roasted Garlic Puree, White Pepper, Salt, and *Maggi Seasoning.
- Thicken if desired with some Cornstarch and cold stock.
- Adjust seasoning as needed.
- Place cooked Barley into cups or bowls (use as much as desired) and ladle hot soup over the Barley.
- Serve immediately.

Serves 6-8

1 cup	Carrots (diced)
1 cup	Celery (diced)
1 cup	Onions (diced)
1 cup	Turnips (diced)
2 T	Olive Oil
2 qt	*Rich Beef Stock
1 lb	Cooked Beef (diced)
1/2 lb	Pearled Barley (cooked, drained and cooled)
To taste	Roasted Garlic puree
To taste	Beef paste

To taste	Ground White Pepper
To taste	Kosher Salt
To taste	*Maggi Seasoning
2-4 T each	Cornstarch and cold stock mixed together

* Rich Beef Stock: Recipe can be found in our "Take Stock" on page 129.

* Roasted Garlic Puree: Take 2 bulbs of fresh garlic peeled to 1 pint of olive oil and place in a sauce pot on medium heat until the garlic turns to teddy bear brown. Strain garlic cloves from oil and cool. Refrigerate the garlic and puree before use in a blender or food processor. Garlic flavored oil can be used for salad dressing or sautéing.

* Maggi Seasoning: Can be purchased from most grocery stores that sell spices.

Broccoli Cheese

I guess it could be true in most family kitchens today that if you put "cheese" on any food the kids will surely eat it. It truly sends me back to the days of wading through the buffet line to replace pans of food to famished patrons as they peered through the sneeze guards waiting for me to put the serving spoons back in their proper place in the Buffet line of endless food. I was a food runner at a buffet restaurant just biding my time until I was able to work my way into the kitchen. Inevitably the cook I replaced often overcooked the broccoli and most vegetables for that matter. I couldn't understand how this guy could kill the broccoli until it was yellow and then proceed by pulling a number 10 can from the pantry, open up the can and pour the whole works over the top of the vegetables and push it over to me and say, "It's ready." Now, at the time I was a pretty good ball player with large agile, hands but, somehow I hit that kitchen door and spilled that pan of cheese covered-yuk all over the floor. I couldn't imagine how I could lose my grip on the pan but, I did. So he scolded me (that's putting it mildly) and said, "Now, you cook the next pan" of which I would sheepishly reply, "Ok." This was my chance to properly steam the veggies and generously cover them with a hot cheese sauce. There are not many opportunities today to get away with that kind of stunt, but the kitchen manager took notice that the Broccoli with Cheese sauce looked great that day. In the days that followed Brian quietly left the restaurant to resume his college studies and I was promoted to vegetable cook, still in high school but anxiously awaiting everyday for the bell to ring the end of the school day so I could get to work and learn new cooking techniques.

- I like to start this soup similar to the rest by sautéing Onions in a little Butter along with fresh *Broccoli florets and stems (if the stems are tender and not woody.)
- Cook this about 5 minutes and introduce the *Golden Chicken Stock.
- Bring the contents of the pot up to a slow boil and reduce the heat to simmer.
- Cook for 20-25 minutes.
- Pour in Heavy Cream and allow the soup to reach simmering stage.
- Season the soup with Chicken paste, Ground White Pepper and Salt.
- Thicken with Cornstarch and cold stock if desired.
- Bring to a simmer again and adjust seasoning to taste.
- Remove soup from heat and stir in a combination of grated Parmesan, Monterey Jack, and Sharp Cheddar Cheese.
- Ladle soup over cooked bite-size *Broccoli florets and garnish with *Garlic Croutons and a little more Cheese.
- Serve immediately

Serves 6-8

* Be sure to reserve some of the florets to cook and cool separately as a final garnish.

1 cup	Onions (sliced)
4 T	Butter
2 lb	Fresh Broccoli (cut up pieces and stems)
2 qt	*Golden Chicken Stock
1 pint	Heavy Cream
To taste	Chicken paste
To taste	Ground White Pepper
To taste	Kosher Salt
2-4 T each	Cornstarch and Cold stock
1 cup each	Grated Parmesan, Sharp Cheddar and Monterey Jack Cheeses

* Golden Chicken Stock: Recipe can be found in our "Take Stock" section on Page 136.

* Garlic Croutons: Toss some Bread cubes with crust removed in melted Garlic flavored Butter in a stainless steel bowl. Season the cubes with Salt and White Pepper and toss again to coat evenly. Transfer the cubes to a sheet pan and bake in a 400° F. oven for 5-10 minutes or until they are golden brown. Remove the tray from the oven and serve with soup as a garnish.

Chicken and Shrimp Creole

A big "shout out" to my friends in New Orleans' for the inspiration behind this great soup. Seems like about every February, I get a call or email from an associate for a recipe they need for the upcoming Mardi Gras Celebration. Well, usually two events precipitate that action: Punxatawny Phil sees his shadow and those of us who are not fans have to bear the brunt of 16 more weeks of basketball on all the prime channels. (ugh!) So as I sit in my ice fishing hut, trying to entice that 8 lb. Brown Trout swimming 12 feet below me to bite, I'm thinking once again of food and how I can deliver a recipe other than the same old Gumbo, Jambalaya, or well, you get the idea. As sure as that Trout bites my baited line I'm reeling in on a great soup that will match up very well with the rest of the Fat Tuesday offerings. Oh by the way, the Brown Trout you see pictured is only 4.5 lbs. amazing how the water magnifies the size of the fish when looking through the aquarium-like portal inside my ice hut. With most good recipes this is one you will enjoy putting together and eating.

- In a stock pot start with the Oil and Flour over medium heat stirring constantly to make a dark chocolate colored *Roux.
- This may take 25-30 minutes so be patient it is worth your time.
- Introduce the *Holy Trinity and season with *Cajun seasoning, Gumbo File Powder, and Ground Black Pepper.
- Cook until the vegetables are soft about 4-6 minutes.
- Add the *Golden Chicken Stock and cook for 10 minutes.
- Stir in diced cooked Chicken, *Tasso Ham, diced Tomatoes, Okra, Rice, and cooked Shrimp.
- Cook and stir occasionally to allow the Rice to cook until tender about 15-20 minutes.
- Once Rice is cooked, adjust seasoning as needed.
- Finish with chopped fresh Parsley and serve.

Serves 6-8

3-1/4 qt	*Golden Chicken Stock
1 cup	Celery (diced)
1 cup	Onion (diced)
1 cup	Green Pepper (diced)
1 cup	Tasso Ham (diced)
1 cup	Tomato (diced)
1 cup	Okra (diced)
1 cup	Long grain Rice
2 cups	Shrimp (cooked and diced)

I tsp	Gumbo File Powder
To Taste	Kosher Salt
To Taste	White Pepper
I tsp	Fresh Parsley (chopped)
2 T	Olive Oil
3 T each	Corn Starch and stock

*CAJUN SPICE RECIPE

2 oz.	Cayenne Pepper
8 oz.	Spanish Paprika
2 oz.	Ground Black Pepper
2 oz.	Ground White Pepper
2 oz.	Dried Oregano
2 oz.	Dried Thyme
4 oz.	Onion Powder
4 oz.	Garlic Powder
8 oz.	Kosher Salt

* Golden Chicken Stock: Recipe can be found in our "Take Stock" section on page 136.

* Roux: Equal amounts of melted Butter or Oil and Flour cooked together and used as a thickening agent for soups and stocks.

* Holy Trinity: A Cajun term derived from the Christian faith of Father, Son, and Holy Spirit. In this case the vernacular is Celery, Onion, and Green Pepper.

* Tasso Ham: Found at your local butcher or specialty store.

Chicken Noodle

The all-time undisputed champion and favorite "feel good and good for you" soup. I guarantee when you make this recipe the kids will think you're the best cook on the planet. Be sure to prepare lots of noodles if your dinky doos loved them as much as our kids did. Some of my fondest memories with our 2 boys were when they "helped" Dad make food. We called our kitchen the "Baloney Palace" where fresh noodles and "fall-apart meat" were prepared. Even if I was just making dinner or preparing for a holiday feast, my junior chefs were at my side wondering what this crazy chef was going to come up with to eat and how they could help. Our tradition was to make homemade noodles on Christmas Eve. Just follow your favorite Pasta dough recipe, roll out the dough to a 1/4 inch thickness and cut the Noodles wide (as the width of your index finger.) Since these are fresh Noodles they can be plunged into boiling salted water and cooked in 4-5 minutes. After the noodles are cooked they can be placed into an ice bath and "shocked" to stop the cooking process and refrigerated for up to 1 week. This works if your schedule is tight.

The next step in this parade is to make the rest of the soup. My oldest son Josh is an accomplished professional cook in Colorado Springs and has worked in our restaurant kitchen affectionately named, Nana Longo's. Our other son Geoff has worked in the kitchen alongside of me as well. He resides in L.A. as an aspiring actor, color-guard coach for a world-class marching corps and manages a clothing outlet. His schedule makes even me tired. Both boys will occasionally text or call to inquire about a recipe for a dinner he is working on to which I gladly lend suggestions.

- For this recipe pour in some *Golden Chicken Stock, diced Carrot, Leek, and Onion bring the contents of the pot to a *Slow boil.
- For added flavor, place a *Sachet bag in the stock to include 1 Bay Leaf, 1 Sprig of fresh Thyme and 1/4 Sprigs of Rosemary, and crushed Black Pepper.
- Reduce the pot to a simmer for 20-30 minutes.
- Remove the bag and add cooked, diced Chicken.
- Season the soup with Chicken Paste to fortify the stock, Ground White Pepper and cook for 5-7 minutes additionally.
- Thicken slightly with Arrowroot Powder and Cold stock.
- I like to allow the vegetables to float in the soup.
- Adjust the seasoning if needed.
- Remove the soup from the stovetop and ladle into bowls of cooked Noodles, *Chiffonade of fresh Spinach, and sliced Scallions.
- Serve immediately.

Serves 6-8

I cup	Carrots (diced)
I cup	Leeks (sliced-white only)
I cup	Onion (diced)
I lb	Chicken (cooked, diced)
2 qt	*Golden Chicken Stock
I each	*Sachet bag: 2 Bay Leaves, Thyme and Rosemary, Black Peppercorns
To taste	Chicken paste
To taste	Ground White Pepper
To taste	Kosher Salt
2-4 T	Arrowroot and cold stock mixed together
2 T	Spinach *Chiffonade
2 T	Green Onion or Scallions (sliced)

* Golden Chicken Stock: Recipe can be found in our "Take Stock" section on page 136.

* Chiffonade: Culinary term for a fine julienne of vegetables for garnish.

* Slow boil: Culinary term for bubbles just breaking the surface of the pot.

* Sachet bag: Culinary term for spices and aromatics tied up into a cheesecloth bag to enhance the flavor of a soup or stock.

Golden Lentil and Sausage

I am neither a borrower nor a Lentil Bean. But I know you will become a big fan of this hearty full-flavored soup. This soup has many options as far as Lentils are concerned. I like the Golden Lentils (sometimes referred to as Yellow Split Peas) but the French and Mediterranean or Middle East Lentils are suitable for this recipe as well. It is recorded in the Old Testament that Esau, who was starving at the time, sold his birthright to his brother Jacob for a "red stew of lentils." That is why Esau's other name is translated to Edom: meaning Red. He thus gave up his position as first born son for Lentil Stew. The bold flavors of this hearty bowl will soon have you asking for a second serving.

- In a stock pot sauté Carrots Celery, Leeks, Onion until tender.
- Add Hambones, soaked Lentils and *Golden Chicken Stock.
- Simmer 20-30 minutes.
- Remove Hambone and add Tomato Puree and roasted Garlic Puree, Lea and Perrins Sauce, Ground White Pepper and Honey Powder.
- Cook for 5-10 minutes more.
- Thicken with Cornstarch and Cold Stock if desired.
- Cook for an additional 5 minutes.
- Adjust seasoning if needed and add cooked sliced Italian Sausage.
- Ladle soup into a bowl, garnish as you wish and serve with some grilled Flat Bread.

Serves 6-8

I cup	Carrots (diced)
I cup	Celery (diced)
I cup	Leeks (sliced)
I cup	Onion (diced)
I each	Ham bone
3-1/4 qt	*Golden Chicken Stock
2 T	Tomato Puree
2 tsp	*Roasted Garlic Puree
2 cups	Golden Lentils (washed and soaked over night in fridge)
1/2 lb	Italian Link Sausage (cooked)
2 T	Cornstarch (mixed with equal parts of stock)
2 T	Olive Oil
To taste	Kosher Salt
To taste	Ground White Pepper
To taste	Honey Powder
To taste	Lea & Perrins Sauce

* Golden Chicken Stock: Recipe can be found in our "Take Stock" section on page 136.

* Roasted Garlic Puree: Take 2 bulbs of fresh garlic peeled to 1 pint of olive oil and place in a sauce pot on medium heat until the garlic turns to teddy bear brown. Strain garlic cloves from oil and cool. Refrigerate the garlic and puree before use in a blender or food processor. Garlic flavored oil can be used for salad dressing or sautéing.

Minestrone

The true anchor of Italian cuisine is to start with a good soup. I've heard it said that soup nourishes the body and lifts the soul. It seems like every other day in my little Nana's kitchen she was forever with a pot of stock simmering on the stovetop. The smells and the aromas of other foods cooking always clashed in a harmonious kind of theme. She was always snapping Peas or some kind of Bean sitting in the shade on the lawn or front porch during the cool of the evening. I would join her to keep her company and lend a hand at the labor of love. These were the times when it seemed like food was more than just sustenance. Some of our most joyous and sorrow-filled times revolved around the family table. I believe it is because I could always look into each of my sibling's eyes and tell if he or she had been through a rough day. We found great solace as a family around that table of food and not necessarily for food's sake. As the years went by we rejoiced with new additions to the family and celebrated the passing of a loved one. We could have agreements and disagreements around the table as well on birthdays, holidays, weddings and funerals. But, one subject that all my family could agree on is that we ate very well at little Nana's table of bounty. This particular soup had very many adaptations over the years, largely due to what was available at the time. So we'll call this the base recipe and you can adapt and customize it how you choose. Buono Apetito!

- In a stock pot sauté Carrot, Celery, Onion, Turnip, Zucchini, and Tomatoes.
- Cook the vegetables in Olive Oil on medium heat until they are tender (4-6 mins.)
- Sprinkle in some dried Oregano, Basil, and *Roasted Garlic Puree.
- Cook for 5 minutes to give the spices a chance to "bloom."
- Pour in *Golden Chicken Stock, soaked White Beans.
- Bring the contents of the pot to a slow boil.
- Reduce the heat to a simmer and cook until the beans are tender (about 30-35 mins.)
- Once the beans are cooked add diced Potato and cook about 10-15 minutes more until the Potatoes are tender.
- Season the soup with Chicken Paste, Ground White Pepper and *Tomato Juice Cocktail.
- Allow the soup to return to a slow boil.
- Thicken soup with some Cornstarch and cold stock.
- Add diced Green Cabbage, any cooked diced meat and remove from the stovetop.
- Stir in a generous amount of grated Pecorino-Romano cheese.
- Ladle soup into bowls containing cooked spaghetti and garnish with a *Chiffonade of fresh Spinach. Serve immediately.

Serves 6-8

I cup	Carrots (diced)
I cup	Celery (diced)

I cup	Onion (diced)
I cup	Turnip (diced)
I cup	Tomato (diced)
I cup	Zucchini (diced)
2 T	Basil Leaves (dried)
2 T	Oregano (dried)
1/2 lb	Potatoes (peeled and diced)
I lb	White Beans (soaked in water overnight in the refrigerator)
4 T	*Roasted Garlic Puree
I lb	*Meat (cooked, diced)
2 qt	*Golden Chicken Stock
2 cups	*Tomato Juice Cocktail
To taste	Chicken Paste
To taste	Ground White Pepper
To taste	Kosher Salt
2-4 T	Cornstarch and cold stock mixed together
2 T	Spinach *Chiffonade
8 oz	Spaghetti (cooked)
4-6 oz	Pecorino-Romano Cheese

* Golden Chicken Stock: Recipe can be found in our "Take Stock" section on page 136.

* Chiffonade: Culinary term for a fine julienne of vegetables for garnish.

* Slow boil: Culinary term for bubbles just breaking the surface of the pot.

* Tomato Juice Cocktail: Such as V-8.

* Meat: Any cooked protein of your choice.

* Bloom: Culinary term-to allow the spices to heat up and intensify in flavor.

* Roasted Garlic Puree: Take 2 bulbs of fresh garlic peeled to I pint of olive oil and place in a sauce pot on medium heat until the garlic turns to teddy bear brown. Strain garlic cloves from oil and cool. Refrigerate the garlic and puree before use in a blender or food processor. Garlic flavored oil can be used for salad dressing or sautéing.

Old Fashion Bean

I've *bean* waiting to share this recipe with everyone that loves Beans. Be it Northern, Cannellini, or even Black-eyed beauties they all add good flavor to this seasoned stock. Similar to the other bean soup recipes this one does have Leeks and Onions paired together with diced Celery and Onion. When our family made the big move to Colorado from Iowa I had come out to spend the summer with little Nana ahead of the family. So for nearly 3 months I came to enjoy the company of cousins and aunts and uncles from my Mom's side of the family. Now, most of them were in fact farmers so when it came to eating it was a "mixed bag" of earthly goodness. I learned to butcher, irrigate crops, ride horses, brand cattle, and pick vegetables in the fields alongside the immigrant work force from south of El Paso. Everything on the farm had a use, nothing was wasted. So when Nana asked me to bring home some soup bones or hocks from the hogs we butchered, I knew what she wanted. These would be rinsed in cold water, placed in a brine solution of Brown Sugar, Salt and Water then left to soak for 2-3 days. Then the *hocks were placed in an open hearth oven outside, which was located next to the cistern, where they were then "smoked" for 6-8 hours. This oven was used for all of the cooking needs during the hot summer days in Blende, Colorado.

- The smoked Shanks go into a stock pot along with Carrots, Celery, Leeks, and Onions.
- Allow this to cook for 5-10 minutes.
- Introduce soaked Beans, *Rich Beef Stock and a *Sachet bag with 2 Bay Leaves, 1 Sprig of fresh Thyme, and 1 tablespoon of crushed Black Peppercorns.
- Bring the contents of the pot up to a *slow boil.
- Reduce to a simmer and cook for 30-40 minutes until the Beans are tender. Please don't email me about the term *al dente*. This is an inexperienced cook's excuse for not cooking food to the proper texture. If the Beans are crunchy they are not cooked! Keep that in mind the next time you cook fresh vegetables.
- Remove Ham shanks and Sachet bag, add diced cooked Ham and trim any meat from the shanks and add to the soup as well.
- Season the soup with Salt, Ground White Pepper, Lea and Perrins Sauce, and Maggi seasoning. I like to strain out about half of the Beans to puree and then return to the pot.
- Allow the heat to return and add just enough Heavy Cream (1-2 cups) to add some richness to the soup.
- Adjust seasoning if needed, finish with chopped fresh Parsley and serve immediately.

Serves 6-8

1 cup	Celery (diced)
1 cup	Carrots (diced)
1 cup	Onion (diced)

I cup	Leeks (sliced white-part only)
I-2 each	Ham hocks (smoked)
I lb	White Beans (soaked overnight in refrigerator)
2-1/2 qt	*Rich Beef Stock
I pint	Heavy Cream
Sachet bag	2 Bay leaves, fresh Thyme sprig, Black Peppercorns (crushed)
2 T	Fresh Garlic (crushed)
To taste	Ground White Pepper
To taste	Kosher Salt
To taste	Lea and Perrins Sauce
To taste	*Maggi Seasoning
2 T	Fresh Parsley (chopped)

* Rich Beef Stock: Recipe can be found in our "Take Stock" section on page 129.

* Maggi Seasoning: Can be found in most spice sections of any food outlet.

* Smoked Hocks: Can be found at any good grocer or butcher shop or take fresh hocks and brine in a solution of I part Brown Sugar to I part Kosher Salt to 4 parts water in the refrigerator for 2-3 days. Use a portable outdoor smoker or charcoal grill with water soaked wood chips such as Hickory and smoke for 6-8 hours with the lid closed. Portable outdoor smokers can be found at most outdoor-type outlets. Get one and have some fun.

* Slow boil: Culinary term for bubbles just breaking the surface of the pot.

* Sachet bag: Culinary term for spices and aromatics tied up into a cheesecloth bag to enhance the flavor or a soup or stock.

Oxtail Soup

As far back as ancient times the ox has been in the spotlight of many historical events. In some cultures the ox is revered as a symbol of good fortune. In biblical times during the plight of the Israelites, soon after their Exodus from Egypt, Moses came down from the Mountain of God to discover the people, along with his brother Aaron, had built for themselves an image of a golden calf. Today, in some Eastern religious beliefs the ox is so valuable it is still used as a form of currency. What is the difference between an ox and regular beef cattle, you might ask? An ox is a castrated bull of the Bovine family tree. Certainly the prime cuts of the animal are highly prized, but the golden nugget for this soup is the tail.

A simple method for cooking the tail piece is to cut the tail in 2 inch portions, dredge them in some seasoned Flour and sauté them in a little Olive Oil until they are browned on both sides. Once this is done, simply braise the pieces in some stock and vegetables until tender.

- For this recipe we will start with a dice of Carrots, Celery, Leeks and Onions in some Olive Oil until the vegetables are tender.
- Introduce some *Rich Beef Stock or *Oxtail Stock and a Sachet bag containing: 2 Bay Leaves, 1 Sprig of fresh Thyme and 1/2 Sprigs of Rosemary, Black Peppercorns (crushed.)
- Bring the contents of the pot to a *slow boil for 30-40 minutes.
- Remove the sachet bag and add cooked diced Beef or Oxtail pieces.
- Season the soup with Beef Paste, Ground White Pepper, Lea and Perrins Sauce, and Kosher Salt.
- Thicken the soup with some Arrowroot Powder and cold stock if desired.
- Allow soup to cook for 5 minutes more.
- Adjust seasoning and remove from stovetop.
- Ladle the soup into bowls or cups.
- Finish with some fresh chopped Chervil and a splash of fresh Lemon juice and serve immediately.

Serves 6-8

1 cup	Carrots (diced)
1 cup	Celery (diced)
1 cup	Onion (diced)
1 lb	Beef (cooked, diced) or Oxtails
2 qt	*Rich Beef Stock or *Oxtail Stock
1 each	Sachet bag: 2 Bay Leaves, Thyme and Rosemary, Black Peppercorns

2 T	*Roasted Garlic Puree
To taste	Beef Paste
To taste	Ground White Pepper
To taste	Kosher Salt
To taste	Lea and Perrins Sauce
2-4 T	Arrowroot Powder and cold stock mixed together

* Rich Beef Stock: Recipe can be found in our "Take Stock" section on page 129.

*Oxtail Stock: Recipe can be found in our "Take Stock" section on page 130.

* Roasted Garlic Puree: Take 2 bulbs of fresh Garlic peeled to 1 pint of Olive Oil and place in a sauce pot on medium heat until the Garlic cloves turns to teddy bear brown. Strain the Cloves from the Oil and cool. Refrigerate the Garlic and puree in a blender or food processor as needed. The remaining Garlic flavored Oil can be used for salad dressing or sautéing.

Philadelphia Pepper Pot

Give me liberty or give this classic. I love the earthiness of this soup. Hearty is truly a good way to describe the flavor of Potatoes, Beef Tripe, Onions and Green Peppers. Those ingredients are a meal in itself. I know you haven't heard me say that before; a soup as a meal . . . You betcha! Did I forget to mention the fresh Spatzle? I think that really sends this soup over the top. Be sure to cook the Tripe a day ahead of time. Tripe is much easier to trim and dice when it is fully cooked and cooled.

- In a stock pot with 4 tablespoons of Butter sauté the *Holy Trinity until the vegetables are tender.
- Add the Potatoes and *Rich Beef Stock and cook until the Potatoes are tender but not mushy.
- Season the soup with Salt, Ground White Pepper, Beef Paste and *Maggi Seasoning.
- Thicken if desired with Cornstarch and Stock.
- Adjust seasoning if needed.
- Ladle hot soup over cooked Spatzle which has been placed in the bottom of the bowl.
- Garnish with fresh chopped Chervil and serve.

Serves 6-8

I cup	Celery (diced)
I cup	Green pepper (diced)
I cup	Onion (diced)
I lb	Potatoes (peeled and diced)
4 T	Butter
2qt	*Rich Beef Stock
I lb	*Beef Tripe (cooked and diced)
To taste	Ground White Pepper
To taste	Kosher Salt
To taste	Beef Paste
To taste	*Maggi seasoning
2-3 T each	Cornstarch and cold stock mixed together
I lb	*Spatzle Noodles (cooked)
2 T	Chervil (chopped)

* Holy Trinity: A Cajun term derived from the Christian faith of Father, Son, and Holy Spirit. In this case the vernacular is Celery, Onion, and Green Pepper.

* Maggi Seasoning: Can be found in most spice sections of any food outlet.

* Rich Beef Stock: Recipe can be found in our "Take Stock" section on page 129.

Spatzle

The Spatzle or little noodles can be made a day or two ahead of time.

- In a stainless steel mixing bowl place 1 lb. of All-Purpose Flour.
- Make a well in the middle of the Flour to hold the 4 large Eggs, 1/2 tsp. of Salt and 1/4 tsp. of Nutmeg.
- Mix together by hand using a wooden spoon.
- Slowly add 1 cup of Milk and mix to achieve a pudding-type viscosity. If the mix is too thick, add some more Milk.
- Press this through a colander into a pot of boiling stock. The *Noodles* will cook almost instantly. Make sure to press all the dough into the stock.
- Remove the colander and stir the Noodles to ensure even cooking.
- Strain and cool in an ice bath to stop the cooking process. We Chefs call this method *shocking*. You will be shocked to realize you just made fresh home made noodles! Yeah!

Beef Tripe

- Prepare the tripe by simmering pieces up to 1 lb. in 1 gallon of boiling *Rich Beef Stock to which 1 cup of Flour has been added. The Flour will help to catch the impurities while the Tripe cooks.
- Cook until the Tripe is tender (2-3 hours) to pierce easily with a fork.
- Remove from the stock and cool before refrigerating.

Scotch Broth

Make no mistake my friends without a doubt William Wallace and his clan were eating this soup long before we even knew there were Highlands in Scotland. Between the Lox and the Haggis this has got to be one of my personal favorites. With each spoonful you may find yourself transported back to a rugged mountain cleft with just enough room for a fire to cook and a place to make your bed for the night. I can picture the small cauldron bubbling slowly as the wind blows along the gloaming. Tasting that first spoonful of flavorful broth, Lamb Meat and vegetables exploding in my mouth is overwhelming, then the warm satisfaction overtaking the chill in my bones all the way to my toes. Begorah! This soup is as rugged and majestic as the city of Edinburg and the great folks that inhabit the country. Without a doubt this is one bowl o'broth you'll want to share with your friends when that North wind howls.

- I like to start with a dice of Carrots, Celery, Onions, Turnip, and Rutabaga sautéed in a little Butter on medium heat.
- Cook the vegetables until they are tender then introduce a combination of *Rich Beef Stock and *Lamb Stock.
- Bring the pot up to a slow boil.
- Reduce the heat to a simmer.
- Cook for 25-30 minutes.
- Add some *Tomato Juice Cocktail, Kosher Salt, Ground White Pepper and cook for 5 minutes more.
- Thicken with some Arrowroot Powder or Cornstarch and Cold stock.
- Add cooked, diced Beef and Lamb to the soup.
- Cook to heat the meat thoroughly.
- Adjust seasoning if needed remove from the stovetop.
- Sprinkle with some chopped fresh Chervil, and ladle into cups or bowls and serve.

Serves 6-8

I cup	Carrots (diced)
I cup	Celery (diced)
I cup	Onion (diced)
I cup	Rutabaga (diced)
I cup	Turnip (diced)
4 T	Butter
I qt	*Rich Beef Stock
I qt	*Lamb Stock
2 cups	Tomato Juice cocktail
I lb each	Beef and Lamb (cooked and diced)

To taste	Ground White Pepper
To taste	Kosher Salt
2-4 T	Arrowroot Powder or Cornstarch and
	Cold stock mixed together

* Tomato Juice Cocktail: Such as V-8.

* Rich Beef Stock: Recipe can be found in our "Take Stock" section on page 129.

* Lamb Stock: Recipe can be found in our "Take Stock" section on page 131.

Split Pea with Ham

I can think of three words to describe this classic of all classic soups: *hearty, flavorful* and *timeless*. By all accounts this is the one soup I look for when traveling on the road and the "hunger monger" starts to talk. When it comes to comfort food, I usually think of this soup. I can recall some 40 years ago now playing in the snow-bound hills of Iowa where I was born. My brother Pete and I would meet up with the neighborhood boys with our sleds and toboggans in tow to the big hill at Shawnee Park. The snow was deep, the wind had a bite to my ears but we would sled up and down that hill for hours until we were nearly frostbitten and then hurry home to mugs of hot split-pea soup. My Mom is still a very good cook to this day, but more importantly she is still a good Mom and Grandmom who knows how to take care of her kids. While the other boys were drinking hot cocoa at their homes, Pete and I were eating this great soup that Mom had made. The credit goes to Mom on this soup but, I have exercised some professional prerogative, being a chef.

- Begin with some smoky Ham shanks purchased from your butcher.
- Place them in a stock pot along with diced Carrots, Celery and Onion with some Butter.
- Let the vegetables and the shanks cook for about 5 minutes.
- Pour in the *Golden Chicken Stock, soaked Split-Peas, Bay Leaves, roasted Garlic Puree.
- Bring the contents of the pot up to a moderate boil for 35-40 minutes until the Peas are cooked and tender.
- Remove the Bay Leaves and the Ham shanks.
- Add diced cooked Ham.
- Season the soup with Ham Paste to fortify the stock, Ground White Pepper, and Kosher Salt.
- Thicken the soup if desired with some Cornstarch and Cold Stock mixed together. I like thick soups that give a feeling of fullness and the "mouth-feel" is the kicker for me.
- Cook the soup for about 5 minutes more.
- Adjust seasoning if needed and remove from the stovetop.
- Ladle the soup into mugs or bowls and serve immediately with some good Bread.

Serves 6-8

1 each	Ham shank
1 cup	Carrots (diced)
1 cup	Celery (diced)
1 cup	Onion (diced)
1 lb	Split Peas (soaked over night in water in refrigerator)

2-1/2 qt	*Golden Chicken Stock
2 each	Bay Leaves
4 T	*Roasted Garlic Puree
1 lb	Ham (cooked and diced)
To taste	Ham Paste
To taste	Ground White Pepper
To taste	Kosher Salt
2-4 T	Cornstarch and Cold Stock mixed together

* Golden Chicken Stock: Recipe can be found in our "Take Stock" section on page 136.

* Roasted Garlic Puree: Take 2 bulbs of fresh Garlic peeled to 1 pint of Olive Oil and place in a sauce pot on medium heat until the Garlic Cloves turn to teddy bear brown. Strain the Cloves from the Oil and cool. Refrigerate the Garlic and puree in a blender or food processor as needed. The remaining garlic flavored Oil can be used for salad dressing or sautéing.

Tomato Leek

After many, many, recipes we have come to the source of inspiration for this book. It was 1989 and I was working for another man with a unique name. Angel was a mountain of a man from the "Big Island." Very generous and very well versed on dining trends. I was responsible for the sauté station 5 days a week. My responsibilities were to set-up my line, prep for the days' business and prepare a soup of the day. The challenge, as Angel put it, was to pull a soup out of . . . well, let's just say come up with a good soup before 11:00 a.m. each day so he could taste it and put his stamp of approval on it. As it goes, the delivery trucks seemed to always run late when we needed the day's catch or even ingredients for soup and other menu items. I looked long and hard in that nearly barren cooler only to find a 1/2 case of Tomatoes and about 6 Leeks. You know, necessity truly is the mother of invention. Thank you, author unknown, for those great words of encouragement. So with those few ingredients I had the courage to create a soup that to this day is still a house favorite at Angel's place. This was also the first time I received some monetary encouragement from a restaurant manager who appreciated the effort. I worked for Angel about a year and then moved onto my first assignment as an Executive Chef. I developed more than enough good training and skill-sets to become a Chef of a major Conference Center in Colorado Springs. Lot's of kudos to all people from all nationalities and skill levels that were open and willing to assist me in achieving my goal as Certified Executive Chef. Thank You! Thank You! And Thank You!

- In a stock pot sauté sliced Leeks in butter on medium heat.
- Cook them until they are *melted*.
- Add fresh chopped Tomatoes, *Golden Chicken Stock, and Tomato Puree.
- Allow the contents of the pot to reach a slow boil and then reduce the heat to a slow simmer.
- Toss in a couple of Bay Leaves and cook for 30-35 minutes. I prefer to use Plum Tomatoes (Roma) for this recipe rather than Beefsteak simply because of taste and substance.
- Season the soup to taste with Chicken Paste, Ground White Pepper, Salt, Honey Powder, and minced fresh Garlic.
- Thicken if desired with Cornstarch and Cold stock.
- Adjust seasoning as needed and serve immediately.
Serves 6-8

2 cups	Leeks (sliced)
4 T	Butter
2 lb	Roma or Plum Tomatoes (diced)
2 qt	*Golden Chicken Stock
1 cup	Tomato Puree

To taste	Garlic (minced)
To taste	Ground White Pepper
To taste	Chicken Paste
To taste	Kosher Salt
To taste	Honey Powder
2-4 T each	Cornstarch and Cold Stock mixed together

* Golden Chicken Stock: Recipe can be found in our "Take Stock" section on page 136.

U.S. Senate Bean

What could be more celebrated and certainly hysterical, sorry historical, than one such soup as this. Why, even our nation's leaders would lobby for this bowl of glory. Years ago when our boys were young and my wife Pam and I had some money, we toured our nation's Capitol. Flying from the Mountain Time zone to the Eastern Time zone we really got off our biological clocks in a hurry and found ourselves famished. We walked into a highly celebrated restaurant called the Old . . . . Grill. To my pleasant surprise the soup of the day was U.S. Senate Bean. I dug right in with a big spoon and almost forgot to come up for air. I learned that from my dear old Dad. When the food hit the family table and Grace was said, Dad was gone to the netherworld in whatever was put in front of him. The only time I heard him comment about a meal was when the silver glitter I was using for a class project got mistaken for the Black Pepper. I do take credit for such a stroke of genius placing that glitter in an exact replica of the pepper shaker. Since then, for the better part of the last 30 years my siblings and I have had a good laugh about the glitter incident at the family table. So Hail to Richard our President Dad!

- For this recipe to be pushed through your family congress; Ham shanks are a must for the start of this soup; otherwise you might get the *veto*.
- Place diced Carrots, Celery, and Onion in the pot along with the Shanks and Butter on medium heat.
- Cook until the vegetables are soft.
- Add *Golden Chicken Stock, Bay Leaves, and soaked Northern Beans.
- Allow this to come to a boil, stir occasionally and cook 45-55 minutes until the beans are soft.
- Remove Ham bones and Bay Leaves from pot.
- Add Tomato Juice, Ground Cloves, Allspice, and cook 10 minutes more.
- Adjust seasoning with Salt, Ground White Pepper, Ham Paste and Cider Vinegar.
- Thicken with Cornstarch and Cold stock mixture.
- Garnish with diced cooked Ham and fresh chopped Parsley.

Serves 6-8

I each	Ham Shank
I cup	Carrots (diced)
I cup	Celery (diced)
I cup	Onion (diced)
I lb	Beans (Northern or white soaked over night in water in refrigerator)
2-1/2 qt	*Golden Chicken Stock
2 each	Bay Leaves

2 cups	Tomato Juice
1 lb	Ham (cooked and diced)
To taste	Ham Paste
To taste	Ground White Pepper
To taste	Ground Cloves
To taste	Ground Allspice
To taste	Kosher Salt
To taste	Cider Vinegar
2-4 T	Cornstarch and Cold Stock mixed together
2 T	Parsley (chopped)

* Golden Chicken Stock: Recipe can be found in our "Take Stock" section on page 136.

CONSOMMÉS

Method for all Consommés

- Always start the consommé in a large heavy bottom stock pot.
- Grind the vegetables and garlic separately from the meat.
- Mix the ground meat, vegetables, spices and aromatics, Tomatoes and Egg whites in a stainless steel mixing bowl.
- Pour the Cold stock into the pot.
- Add the mix slowly; once all the mix is in the pot turn on the heat to medium and stir the ingredients in the pot one time.
- As the stock begins to heat up keep an eye on the meat and vegetable mixture. As the temperature increases, the mixture will begin to rise to the top to form a *Raft. That is the main purpose of egg whites is help to clarify the stock.
- Once the *Raft is formed, reduce the temperature to a low setting.
- Allow the pot to remain at a simmer for 4-6 hours or longer if you prefer.

- To strain the consommé properly, remove the pot from the heat source and make a hole the size of a 4 oz. ladle.
- Begin ladling the consommé into a separate container through some *Rinsed cheesecloth covered china cap or fine mesh strainer.
- Once all of the consommé is strained discard the *Raft and place the cooled consommé in the refrigerator for use later or taste for seasoning.
- Pour into cups with your favorite garnish.
- Finish with a splash of Sherry in each cup and serve.

Yield 2 gallons

* Raft: No relation to George—but the formation of the congealed Egg Whites and ground meat and vegetable mix is called a *Raft, because it floats on the top of the stock and filters the consommé.

* Rinsed cheesecloth: Take the cheese cloth out of the package it came in and rinse to remove any sizing material that may have been used in its production. The cold water will also tighten up the holes for better straining.

Beef Consommé

Once you have made a consommé you will feel like there isn't anything left to conquer. I will not embellish the fact that it is more technical but not intimidating. Making a small batch of consommé at a time will boost your cooking confidence one hundred fold. So assemble the ingredients, wash your hands, say a prayer and let's do some consommé. You'll be the hit of the dinner party when the Petit Marmite is served to your family, friends and guests. The method for making consommé is virtually the same for any meat or game. This will be a master recipe with which to interchange the meat or game components with a few subtle nuances that will be in each different consommé recipe listed in this section of the cookbook.

3 gal	*Rich Beef Stock
1/2 cup	Diced tomatoes
1/2 cup	Celery
1/2 cup	Onion
1/2 cup	Carrot
1 lb	Shank meat (fine grind)
2-3 sprigs	Parsley (mainly stems)
2 each	Garlic cloves (crushed)
1 sprig	Thyme leaves
2 each	Bay leaves
1 T	Whole Black Pepper
1 sprig	Rosemary leaves
8-10 each	Egg whites

* Rich Beef Stock: Recipe can be found in our "Take Stock" section on page 129.

Pheasant Consommé

What makes this Consommé so unique is the flavor profile of the bird. Put together a *Pheasant Stock with roasted Pheasant bones. Be sure to use Pheasant meat for the raft mixture preparation of the Consommé as well. This is a great Consommé for a game themed dinner or as a starter for a black tie affair. I like to add some *Brunoise of cooked vegetables and some diced cooked Pheasant meat to the cup. But, use your imagination, after all this is your party! Follow the Beef Consommé recipe for the method of preparation and remember to substitute the Pheasant meat for the Beef Shank meat.

* Pheasant Stock: Recipe can be found in our "Take Stock" section on page 137.

* Brunoise: Culinary term for a very small dice of vegetables for garnish.

Chicken Consommé

Using the *Golden Chicken Stock recipe found in our "Take Stock" section found on page 136 is a must for this preparation. Use ground Chicken meat for the *Raft mixture. Follow the master Consommé recipe to prepare the Consommé.

Below is a list of a few Consommé garnishes I have used for different flavor components and theme dinner starters.

Celestine: Julienne of crepes with fine herbs.

Petit Marmite: Julienne of Carrot, Celery, Turnip, cooked Beef and Chicken.

Aux pates: Cooked Vermicelli.

Julienne: Julienne of cooked vegetables.

Oxtail Consommé

Cut up the Oxtails into 1 inch pieces or between the joints and brown them in the oven with some *Mirepoix. Use the *Rich Beef Stock recipe to complete the stock preparation for the Consommé. The Beef shank meat will suffice for the raft mixture. Follow the master recipe for the Consommé preparation. A good Sherry will finish the Oxtail Consommé quite nicely prior to service. Be sure to garnish the soup with any cooked vegetables and meat you choose.

* Mirepoix: Culinary term for stock pot vegetables such as Carrots, Celery, and Onions.

* Rich Beef Stock: Recipe can be found in our "Take Stock" section on page 129.

CREAM SOUPS

Andalusia

The southernmost region of Spain is Andalusia. Andalusia is also the originator of Gazpacho, which is also featured in this writing. About 2/3 of Spain's olive trees are located in this part of the country. So, as the day laborers were given their ration of Bread and Olive Oil these dear folks would supplement the bounty with all sorts of vegetables to make the infamous sopa. As we have mentioned before, there are many other influences that mold and shape the cuisine of the world and Andalusia is no exception. There is a strong Arab influence since the Mediterranean and Atlantic are nearby. This recipe contains Cumin and Cinnamon which to that end gives the soup a slightly Moorish appeal.

- Start this soup as you might by preparing a Chicken *Veloute Sauce.
- In a stock pot mix equal parts of melted Butter and Flour to form a *Roux.
- Cook this for 5-7 minutes on medium heat until the roux achieves a blonde appearance and slightly nutty aroma.
- Introduce the *Golden Chicken Stock, Tomato Puree and *Tomato Juice Cocktail
- Bring the contents of the pot to a *Slow boil.
- Reduce heat and cook for 30-40 minutes stirring occasionally.
- Season the soup with Chicken Paste, Ground Cumin, Ground Cinnamon, Ground White Pepper, and Salt.
- Cook the soup for an additional 10 minutes.
- Strain through a fine mesh strainer into another soup pot to remove any lumps.
- Return the soup to the stovetop.
- Add roasted diced Potatoes and Tomatoes and cook to heat through.
- Ladle the soup into cups or bowls garnish with fresh ground Black Pepper
- Serve immediately.

Serves 6-8

1 cup	Butter
1 cup	Flour (all-purpose)
1 qt	*Golden Chicken Stock
1 cup	Heavy Cream
1/2 cup	Tomato Puree
1 cup	*Tomato Juice Cocktail
1 cup	Potatoes (diced and roasted)
1/2 cup	Tomatoes (fresh diced, seeded)
1 T	Ground Cumin
1 tsp	Ground Cinnamon
To taste	Chicken Paste
To taste	*Ground Black Pepper
To taste	Kosher Salt

* Ground Black Pepper as a final garnish.

* Veloute: Mother sauce used a base for soups and sauces.

* Golden Chicken Stock: Recipe can be found in our "Take stock" section on page 136.

* Tomato Juice Cocktail: Such as V-8 juice.

* Slow boil: Culinary term for small bubbles just breaking the surface of the pot.

* Roux: Equal amounts of melted Butter or Oil and Flour cooked together and used as a thickening agent for soups and stocks.

Artichoke and Mushroom

Do you ever find yourself wondering why Arti choked when there was mush room to breathe? Well, chew carefully, catch your breath and get ready to make a great soup for that next family dinner or food affair with friends. I would sit and listen to my Nana on the front porch of the house nearly every night during the summer months as she recalled stories from her past. We would snap beans or shuck fresh Peas for the next days' lunch as she talked about eating such things as Cucumber and Onion sandwiches. Sometimes it was just Onion sandwiches as the Cucumbers needed to be sold at the market. Or the wild Asparagus that grew alongside the irrigation ditches that she would gather and add to an egg mixture to make a Frittata. "This was all the food we had to eat for the week," she exclaimed. She learned to use everything edible that could be found, raised, grown, or hatched on a farm. The day she walked into her kitchen with Artichokes I was already asking to help. She taught me how to clean them to remove the outer leaves and remove the choke. The clean "chokes" were then placed in some simmering Lemon-infused Chicken Stock and cooked slowly until they were tender. This would be the inspiration for me to create the following recipe for this soup. If you're not near a good source of fresh Artichokes, then go ahead and use the canned type. Just make sure the Artichoke Hearts you purchase are not pickled or marinated.

- Once again, I like to roast the Artichokes and the Mushroom in a little Olive Oil on a sheet pan for 20-30 minutes or longer if needed in a 400° F. oven.
- While Arti and the 'Shrooms are roasting make a *Roux in a stock pot.
- Allow this *Roux to cook to a blonde color with a slight nuttiness (5-7 minutes.)
- Pour into the pot *Golden Chicken Stock and any strained liquid reserved from the Artichoke Hearts can.
- Cook and stir to form a thickened sauce *Veloute to reach a *Slow boil for 25-30 minutes on medium heat.
- Season the soup with Chicken Paste, Nutmeg, Cayenne Pepper, fresh Lemon Juice, Honey Powder, Salt, and Ground White Pepper.
- Add some Heavy Cream to the sides of the pot to minimize the *Temperature plunge and bring back to a slow boil.
- Adjust seasoning to taste if needed and pour mixture through a fine mesh strainer to remove any lumps into another soup container and keep hot.
- Introduce the roasted Artichokes and Mushrooms back into the soup and return to stove top to heat through if needed.
- Ladle soup into bowls or cups and serve immediately.

Serves 6-8

1/2 cup	Butter
1/2 cup	Flour (all-purpose)
1-1/2 qt	*Golden Chicken Stock
2 cups	Artichoke Hearts (roasted, chopped)
2 cups	Mushrooms (roasted, chopped)
1 cup	Heavy Cream
To taste	Chicken Paste
To taste	Ground White Pepper
To taste	Cayenne Pepper
To taste	Ground Nutmeg
To taste	Lemon Juice (fresh squeezed)
To taste	Kosher Salt
To taste	Honey Powder

* Golden Chicken Stock: Recipe can be found in our "Take Stock" section on page 136.

* Veloute: Mother sauce used as a base for soups and sauces.

* Slow boil: Culinary term for small bubbles just breaking the surface of the pot.

* Temperature plunge: Occurs when a cold liquid is introduced into a hot liquid slowing down the cooking process.

* Roux: Equal amounts of melted Butter or Oil and Flour cooked together to form a thickening agent for soups and stocks.

Crab and Spinach

This is a very simple soup to put together in a very short time. As mentioned before, if you can use fresh Spinach instead of frozen the results are profound. Canned processed Crab may be a good choice if fresh isn't available, make certain to pick through the entire can of crab to find and discard any pieces of shell, which can be common. I have made the mistake in my haste to pour the crab meat into the soup only to find out a few hours later that one of my restaurant patrons needed to see me personally to point out my poor judgment in time savings. Thankfully, Ken and his wife Sandy, who were loyal customers, were gracious enough to discreetly explain my faux pas and not create too much attention. Incidentally I have found that picking through the fresh Crabs we have prepared need a good picking through as well. One principal I have educated my staff on over the years is to learn from your mistakes by not repeating them again. This is a great soup to pour into a Bread Bowl and serve to your hungry guests.

- In a stock pot sauté some Celery, Leeks, and Onions with butter on medium heat until the vegetables are soft.
- Sprinkle into the pot the same amount of Flour as Butter and cook for 4-6 minutes.
- Introduce the *Fish Stock and cook for 10-15 minutes until the soup thickens.
- Pour in the Heavy Cream around the sides of the pot to minimize *Temperature plunge.
- Bring the soup up to *Slow boil and cook for 10 more minutes.
- Add the Crab and Spinach to the soup season with Sea Salt and Ground White Pepper to taste.
- Ladle the soup into cups or Bread Bowls and serve immediately.

Serves 6-8

I cup	Celery (sliced)
I cup	Leeks (sliced)
I cup	Onions (sliced)
I lb	Crab (picked clean)
2 lb	Spinach (fresh, de-stemmed)
I qt	*Fish Stock
4 T	Butter
4 T	Flour (all-purpose)
I qt	Heavy Cream
To taste	Ground White Pepper
To taste	Sea Salt

* Fish Stock: Recipe can be found in our "Take Stock" section found on page 133.

* Temperature plunge: Occurs when a cold liquid is introduced into a hot liquid slowing down the cooking process.

* Slow boil: Culinary term for small bubbles just breaking the surface of the pot.

* Roux: Equal amounts of melted Butter or Oil and Flour cooked together to form a thickening agent for soup and stocks.

Curry Bombay

You can get curried away if you're not careful with this wonderful soup. The flavors explode on your palate with each spoonful of Curry, Coconut, diced cooked Chicken, Scallions, and fresh Cilantro. Would someone just pick me up and curry me away to Kathmandu? My new nephew, Shree from Boston, is Indian and I can't wait to get his opinion on this favorite soup. I once had the pleasure of working with some students from Madras. These were men in their early twenties traveling the world learning to cook among other things, from ancient cultures. This was the foodie club I wanted to belong to. But, with a faithful wife, two well-mannered boys, and a career that would give me a great deal of satisfaction later down the years, I had to turn down the open invitation. But I was pleased when Sunil and the guys would drop me a line and a gift occasionally. Sunil would try his best to buy spices for me and then attempt to bring them into the U.S. At the time it wasn't the U.S. that had the problem but the thievery that was rampant leaving the country of India. I can recall the excited phone call from Sunil when he told me he just purchased all the ingredients for us to make our own blend of Curry. Only to be followed by a solemn voice the next day on the phone telling me the spices were all, well let's just call it confiscated, for I'm sure some customs officers' wife to use when he got home. Nevertheless, I know this recipe will be one you will want to share with others. God love you Sunil and friends, wherever you are today!

- Start this soup in a stock pot with some Onions and *Clarified Butter.
- Sauté the Onions until they are brown and immediately stir in the Curry powder and allow it to bloom (1 minute.)
- Add Flour.
- Stir to form a *Roux. This process will take about 3-4 minutes on low heat.
- Pour in *Golden Chicken Stock, Coconut Milk and Heavy Cream.
- Bring the contents of the pot up to a *Slow boil and cook for 20-30 minutes.
- Thicken the soup with Cornstarch and cold stock to desired viscosity and cook for 6-8 minutes additionally.
- Season soup with Chicken paste to fortify the stock, Ground White Pepper, and Salt.
- Remove the soup from the stovetop.
- Pour the soup through a fine mesh strainer and into another soup pot.
- Return the soup to the heat.
- Toss in chopped fresh Cilantro, sliced Scallions and cooked diced Chicken meat.
- Cook an additional 5 minutes and remove from stovetop.
- Ladle the soup into bowls and garnish with shredded Coconut, diced Tomatoes, chopped Peanuts and diced Bananas. Serve immediately.

Serves 6-8

I cup	Onion (sliced)
4 T	*Clarified Butter
4 T	Flour (all-purpose)
2 T	Madras Curry Powder
I qt	*Golden Chicken Stock
I lb	Chicken (cooked, diced)
I pint	Coconut Milk
I pint	Heavy Cream
2-3 T each	Cornstarch and Cold Stock mixed together
To taste	Chicken Paste
To taste	Ground White Pepper
To taste	Kosher Salt
2 T	Scallions (sliced)
2 T	Cilantro (chopped)
2 T	Tomatoes (seeded, diced)
2 T	Peanuts (chopped)
2 T	Coconut (shredded)
2 T	Banana (diced)

* Golden Chicken Stock: Recipe can be found in our "Take Stock" section on Page 136.

* Slow boil: Culinary term for small bubbles just breaking the surface of the pot.

* Roux: Equal amounts of melted Butter or Fat and Flour cooked together and used as a thickening agent for soups and stocks.

* Clarified Butter: Butter that has been simmered slowly to remove all the milk solids.

George's Potato Cheddar

My father-in-law was a truck driver for decades before he started his own company. He would know, without hesitation, how to direct me from one side of Denver to the other as if his brain had a GPS chip inside. He was a Godly man for whom I have immense respect. For all the years I have had the honor and privilege of talking and learning from George, he has been a gentle, loving and devoted man. He genuinely lived and modeled the Christian life all of his days with very few complaints about anything. So, when he traveled about the towns all over Colorado and the surrounding states as an over-the-road driver, he knew where the best places were to "grab a bite to eat." George was a meat and potatoes kind of guy, but as most folks living in the farming communities of Eastern Colorado, he would say, "You learn to eat what's put in front of you." I have seldom heard him complain about a meal. But, when it came to the discussion of soup, I knew one of his favorites was Potato-Cheddar. So, it is my distinct pleasure to share this "family" recipe with you in honor of the man I respectfully call Dad.

- In a stock pot sauté Leeks and Onions in Butter on medium heat until vegetables are soft.
- Add rough cut Yukon Gold Potatoes and stir the pot.
- Introduce *Golden Chicken Stock, 2 Bay Leaves.
- Cook the contents of the pot on a medium boil until the Potatoes are ready to be smashed (25-35 minutes.)
- Remove Bay Leaves and pour Heavy Cream down the sides of the pot to minimize *Temperature plunge.
- Bring pot back to a boil and remove from the stovetop.
- With an immersion blender or food mill, puree Potato mixture until smooth and velvety.
- Return soup to the stovetop and adjust the viscosity with more Stock or Cream to achieve the proper mouth-feel.
- Season the soup with Chicken Paste, Ground White Pepper and Salt to taste.
- Cook for an additional 5-7 minutes stirring the pot so the soup doesn't scorch.
- Remove from stovetop and stir in as much shredded Cheddar Cheese as you like.
- Ladle the soup into bowls, garnish with cooked crumbled Bacon, snipped fresh Chives or my favorite *Crispy Leeks and serve immediately.

Serves 6-8

I cup	Leeks (sliced)
I cup	Onions (sliced)
4 T	Butter
2 lb	Yukon Gold Potatoes (rough-cut)

2-1/2 qt	*Golden Chicken Stock
2 each	Bay Leaves
1 qt	Heavy Cream
To taste	Chicken Paste
To taste	Ground White Pepper
To taste	Kosher Salt
2-3 cups	Cheddar (sharp, shredded)
2 T	Chives (snipped)

* Crispy Leeks: Soak julienne Leeks in Buttermilk for 10 minutes, drain well, dredge in seasoned Flour and fry in Olive Oil until the Leeks are golden brown. Remove them from the hot Oil onto paper towels to cool and serve.

* Temperature plunge: Occurs when a cold liquid is introduced into a hot liquid slowing down the cooking process.

* Golden Chicken Stock: Recipe can be found in our "Take Stock" section on page 136.

Spinach and Ham

A special announcement to all my soup loving friends; for the love of the sailor man do not use canned or frozen Spinach for this recipe as a short-cut or I'll personally turn myself into Bluto and come find you. Make sure to de-stem the fresh Spinach and wash it well. Add some great quality Ham and the crowd will start forming outside your house. Olive Oyle might even make an appearance, LOL. Ugh! Ugh! Ugh! Ugh! I know I'll get email for this one and no offense to my Spinach grower-type friends; so here I go anyway.

Spinach has a great flavor and I feel like we can mostly agree on that one. I have used it with fresh Strawberries and a Balsamic glaze for a great salad. I have seasoned and creamed it for a great side vegetable as well as sautéed and seasoned for a wonderful accompaniment to a grilled steak. However, Spinach has very little nutritive value and I would like to think the sailor-man ate it because he liked it; not for the muscle building strength it somehow mysteriously possessed. In conclusion, let's chalk-it up to a great marketing scheme and leave it at that ok?

- As with most cream soups, start with a stock pot with melted Butter and sauté some sliced Onion and chopped Garlic on medium heat until the Onions are cooked but not browned (4-6 minutes.)
- Sprinkle the same amount of Flour into the pot as the Butter and cook the mixture, stirring constantly as the *Roux forms and turns a blonde color with a slight nutty aroma.
- Stir in the fresh Spinach and *Golden Chicken Stock. Be sure to keep stirring the pot occasionally as the soup begins to thicken and cook for 20-30 minutes.
- Pour the Heavy Cream down the sides of the pot to minimize *Temperature plunge.
- Season the soup with Nutmeg, Ham Paste to fortify the stock, Ground White Pepper and Honey Powder.
- Continue cooking for an additional 10-12 minutes.
- Adjust seasoning to taste if needed and add diced cooked Ham to the soup.
- Cook to heat the Ham through (2-3 minutes) and remove the pot from stovetop.
- Ladle into cups or bowls and serve immediately.

Serves 6-8

I cup	Onions (sliced)
2 T	Garlic (chopped)
4 T	Butter
4 T	Flour (all-purpose)
4 lb	Spinach leaves (de-stemmed)
2 qt	*Golden Chicken Stock

1 pint	Heavy Cream
1 lb	Ham (cooked, diced)
To taste	Ham Paste
To taste	Ground Nutmeg
To taste	Ground White Pepper
To taste	Honey Powder

* Golden Chicken Stock: Recipe can be found in our "Take Stock" section on page 136.

* Temperature plunge: Occurs when a cold liquid is introduced into a hot liquid slowing down the cooking process.

* Roux: Equal amounts of melted Butter or Fat and Flour cooked together to form a thickening agent for soups and stocks.

Wild Mushroom

I was reluctant at first to submit a Mushroom Soup recipe when each of us has this immediate brain surge of that hideous-tasting stuff in the red and white labeled can. I understand it has its place among the Green Beans and French Fried Onions during the holidays. I will probably be the first one to dig into the casserole dish sitting alongside that big golden bird on my mother-in-laws dining room table laden with food fit for a king. I can remember Esther's Chicken and Rice casserole vividly along with some other very good dishes. As I have said she is a wonderful cook and between her, and my Little Nana and my mom I learned all the right moves in the kitchen. But, ladies and gentlemen I submit to you that the stuff in the can doesn't have a prayer next to the following recipe. So have some fun with this one and create your own garnishments to personalize the soup.

- I like to use meaty Mushrooms for this recipe such as Crimini or Baby Portabellas. Also, as in previous recipes, I like to roast the Mushrooms to deepen the flavors.
- Coat the Mushrooms lightly with some Olive Oil and a little fresh Thyme.
- Roast them in a 400° F oven for 20-30 minutes until they are roasted and about half of their normal size.
- While the Mushrooms are roasting begin sautéing some Leeks and Shallots in *Clarified Butter until they are soft but not brown (3-4 minutes.)
- Add Flour to the vegetables and stir to form a *Roux.
- Cook and stir until the roux mixture take on a blonde appearance and has a slightly nutty aroma.
- *Deglaze the vegetables with some Sherry followed by some *Golden Chicken Stock, and Heavy Cream.
- Bring the contents of the pot up to a *Slow boil. Allow this to cook for 15-20 mins.
- Thicken the soup with some Cornstarch and cold stock to desired viscosity.
- Reduce the heat to a simmer.
- Add in the mushrooms and season the soup with Chicken Paste to fortify the stock with Ground White Pepper and Salt to taste.
- Cook for an additional 10 minutes adjust seasoning as needed and remove the pot from the stovetop.
- Ladle soup into cups or bowls garnish with *Walnut Pesto and serve immediately. Serves 6-8

I cup	Leeks (sliced, white-part only
2 T	Shallots (chopped)
4 T	Butter (clarified)
4 T	Flour (all-purpose)

1/2 cup	Sherry
2 lb	Mushrooms (Crimini, Portabella, Morels, Oyster)
4 T	Olive Oil (for Mushrooms)
2 qt	*Golden Chicken Stock
1 pint	Heavy Cream
To taste	Chicken Paste
To taste	Ground White Pepper
To taste	Kosher Salt

* Golden Chicken Stock: Recipe can be found in our "Take Stock" section on page 136.

Walnut Pesto

- In a food processor combine Walnuts, Garlic, Parmesan Cheese, Spinach Leaves, and Basil.
- Mix to pulverize and slowly stream Olive Oil into the processor to achieve desired consistency; Pesto should remain somewhat firm to use as a dollop for garnishment.

* Deglaze: Culinary term used for washing the browned bits of food from the inside bottom of a sauce pot or pan using an acid e.g. Wine, juice, stock.

* Clarified Butter: Butter which has been slow simmered on the stovetop to remove all the milk solids leaving just the pure liquid.

* Slow boil: Culinary term for small bubbles just breaking the surface of the pot.

Wild Rice and Chicken

I want to give a big cheer to my friends in Grand Marais Minnesota for this great soup recipe. While traveling up the Superior coast on my way to Walleye heaven; I stopped into a little roadside eatery for a quick bite and this is what I ordered; a creamy, smooth soup with cooked diced Chicken, vegetables and this great tasting grain. That's right, Wild Rice is not technically Rice, it is a grain grown in the marshes. Our Native American friends certainly knew what to do with this great treasure, particularly the Owjibwa or Chippewa tribe. With that soup and some good Bread down the "pipe" I was on my way to catch as many "eyes" as my license would allow. There is a bounty of good eating Fresh Water Fish in our great nation and I believe the Walleye is toward the top of the list. I have used this Wild Rice for many Fish and game-type presentations over the years. So I'm sure you will have no problem formulating your own food ideas once the inspiration of this soup recipe sinks in. I have discovered the best way to start this recipe is to cook the rice separately with some Carrots, Celery, Onion and some Bacon in a pot of Golden Chicken Stock with a Bay Leaf added. Slow simmer the Rice until the Rice is tender to the bite. Remove the Bay Leaf and cover the Rice to keep it warm until service.

- In a stock pot sauté some Celery, Leeks, and Onions in some *Clarified Butter until the vegetables are tender.
- Sprinkle in the same amount of flour to absorb the butter to form a *Roux.
- Cook this vegetable *Roux mix on medium heat and stir to keep the *Roux to a blonde appearance and slight nut-like aroma (6-8 minutes.)
- Stir in the *Golden Chicken Stock whisking to form a thickened sauce.
- Allow this to cook on a slow boil for 25-30 minutes stirring the pot occasionally.
- Pour Heavy Cream down the side of the pot to avoid the *Temperature plunge.
- Chicken Paste to fortify the stock, Ground White Pepper, and Salt to taste.
- Bring the contents of the pot back to a slow boil.
- Add in the diced cooked Chicken and *Cooked Wild Rice.
- Adjust seasoning if needed and remove the pot from the stovetop.
- Ladle the soup into cups or bowls and serve immediately.

Serves 6-8

* Clarified Butter: Butter that has been simmered slowly to remove all the milk solids.

* I suggest adding the Chicken and Rice to the bowl and pouring the soup over top. This way the Rice won't have a chance to over-thicken the soup.

| 1 cup | Celery (diced) |
| 1 cup | Leeks (sliced) |

1 cup	Onion (diced)
4 T	Butter (clarified)
4 T	Flour (all-purpose)
2 qt	*Golden Chicken Stock
1 pint	Heavy Cream
1 lb	Chicken meat (cooked, diced)
To taste	Chicken Paste
To taste	Ground White Pepper
To taste	Kosher Salt

Wild Rice Recipe

1/2 cup	Bacon (diced)
1/4 cup	Carrots (diced)
1/4 cup	Celery (diced)
1/4 cup	Onion (diced)
1 each	Bay Leaf
1/2 lb	Wild Rice
4 cups	*Golden Chicken Stock

- Sauté the Bacon in a sauce pot on medium heat until rendered.
- Add vegetables and Rice.
- Cook for 3-4 minutes.
- Pour in *Golden Chicken Stock, Bay Leaf.
- Reduce heat to simmer and cook until all the stock has absorbed and the Rice begins to plump (some grains will burst.)
- Remove from stovetop and keep warm until needed.

* Golden Chicken Stock: Recipe can be found in our "Take Stock" section on page 136.

* Roux: Equal amounts of melted Butter or fat and Flour cooked together to form a thickening agent for soups and stocks.

GLOBAL FAVORITES

Black Bean Soup

On a cruise to the Bahamas by way of Jamaica; I felt the urge to walk into the ship's kitchen unannounced. Now, I know this was a bold move, but so are the flavors of this wonderful Bean soup that I just have to share with you. Juveen was the lady in the classic chefs' toque who greeted me so casually I didn't feel as if I were intruding. We exchanged pleasantries, and then she asked me what I needed. There was my opening! I explained that I was an Executive Chef from Colorado and wanted to get a glimpse of the kitchen operation. She smiled and replied, "Follow me." She was vivacious and worth following. For the next 2 hours, I felt like I was royalty, hence the name of the cruise line. I was introduced to the Executive Chef and his crew. After a few kind words and Chef talk, Juveen was at my side to resume the tour as the Executive Chef needed to attend to his business. Juveen was the Chef de Potage responsible for the soups and stocks! What a stroke of luck! The Soup du jour for the evening was Puree of Black Bean. On average, she will produce 125 gallons of soup a day! Yah Mon! I wasn't going to take up more of her time so I politely excused myself and found the exit. When the soup came to our table that night I was nearly in a trance as I took the first spoonful. The blend of spices for this soup was really the knockout punch I had hoped to experience. I hope the first spoonful you eat puts your olfactory senses into the next day as well.

- In a stock pot sauté the vegetables and Ham shank with the Garlic in Butter on medium heat (5-6 minutes to soften the vegetables.)
- Pour in *Rich Beef Stock, soaked Black Turtle Beans, and Bay Leaves.
- Bring the contents of the pot up to a moderate boil.
- Cook for 35-45 minutes until beans are soft.
- Remove Ham Shanks and Bay Leaves.
- Pour the Cream down the sides of the pot to minimize *Temperature plunge.
- Cook 5 minutes more before pureeing.
- Return pureed soup to pot.
- Season the soup with Beef Paste to fortify the stock with Allspice, Mace, Ground Cloves, Honey Powder, Cayenne Pepper, Ground White Pepper, and Salt.
- Bring the soup back to a simmer and splash in some good Burgundy.
- Remove the pot from the stovetop and ladle into soup bowls and garnish with diced hard boiled Egg. Serve at once.

Serves 6-8

1 cup	Carrots (diced)
1 cup	Celery (diced)
1 cup	Onion (diced)
1 each	Ham shank

2 T	Garlic (chopped)
2-1/2 qt	*Rich Beef Stock
1 lb	Black Turtle Beans (soaked in water in the refrigerator overnight)
2 each	Bay Leaves
1 pint	Heavy Cream
2 T	Beef Paste
1/2 tsp	Allspice (ground)
1/2 tsp	Mace (ground)
1/2 tsp	Cloves (ground)
1/2 tsp	Cayenne Pepper
To taste	White Pepper (ground)
To taste	Kosher Salt
To taste	Honey Powder
1 cup	Burgundy Wine

* Rich Beef Stock: Recipe can be found in our "Take Stock" section on page 129.

* Temperature plunge: Occurs when a cold liquid is poured into a hot liquid slowing down the cooking process.

Borscht

The Volga may be icy, snow covered in Minsk. So what better reason do you need to make this classic soup? I was challenged to make this soup along with some other Russian dishes for a group of American missionary students preparing to live in the USSR for a year when it was still called the USSR. I am proud to say that the students that left for the mission work wrote me on occasion; explaining to me how much better this soup was than the one some of the Soviet country folk would serve them. Well, I'm glad that soup worked for those students. I have had several students from the former Soviet Union work in my kitchen and I have learned many great recipes and lessons of life from them. In fact, I have had the benefit of working with peoples from all walks of life. This has shaped the way I cook and how I respond to folks from all corners of the globe. It is the fiber that weaves what we call American cuisine today in my humble opinion. For example, I was ready to throw out some fish heads when a student from Malaysia frantically stopped me. He then went about the kitchen gathering vegetables and spices to make a soup out of the discards. I mean to tell you the soup was incredible to say the least. So that day I vowed to become more frugal and open-minded in my cooking style.

- In a stock pot on medium heat sauté Celery, Leeks, and Onions in a little butter.
- Cook the vegetables for 3-4 minutes.
- Introduce a combination of *Duck Stock and *Rich Beef Stock.
- Toss in a *Sachet bag containing: 2 Bay Leaves, small bunch of Parsley stems, I T black Peppercorns, 2 crushed Garlic Cloves, and I Lemon cut in two pieces.
- Allow the soup to come up to a boil and reduce heat to a simmer for 15-20 minutes.
- Remove the sachet bag and add Potatoes, shredded Green Cabbage, *Peeled, rough cut Red Beets, and Tomatoes.
- Continue to cook for 10-15 minutes until the Potatoes and Beets are tender.
- Puree the soup through a food mill or blender.
- Pour the pureed soup back into the pot and season with Beef Paste to fortify the soup, Ground White Pepper and Salt.
- Bring the soup back up to a simmer adjust seasoning if needed.
- Finish with a splash of Apple Cider Vinegar.
- Place cooked pieces of Beef and Duck into a soup cup or bowl, ladle soup over top. Serve immediately.

Serves 6-8

I cup	Celery (sliced)
I cup	Leeks (sliced)
I cup	Onion (sliced)
4 T	Butter

I qt	*Duck Stock
I qt	*Rich Beef Stock
I each	*Sachet bag
I lb	Potatoes (peeled and rough-cut)
I lb	*Red Beets (peeled and rough-cut)
2 each	Tomatoes (medium—rough-cut)
I/2 lb	Green Cabbage (shredded)
I lb	Duck (cooked and diced)
I lb	Beef (cooked and diced)
2 T	Beef Paste
To taste	Ground White Pepper
To taste	Kosher Salt
To taste	Apple Cider Vinegar

* Be sure to wear food handler's gloves when peeling and slicing the Beets or you will have red stained hands for a week.

* Rich Beef Stock: Recipe can be found in our "Take Stock" section on page 129.

* Duck Stock: Recipe can be found in our "Take Stock" section on page 138.

* Sachet Bag: Culinary term for spices and aromatics tied up in a cheesecloth bag to enhance the flavor of a soup or stock.

California Cioppino

Do not start this recipe until you have secured a loaf of authentic San Francisco Sourdough Bread. This soup is really considered a combination of a good red sauce and a beautiful array of fresh Seafood. This is truly a meal in itself by all definition. My Uncle Jimmy would be up at 4:30 a.m. every day. Well, he was a vegetable farmer so he was always an early riser. That may have been why I have always been an early riser as well. Anyway, he would jump into his old pick-up truck and down the road he would go, with me riding the infamous "shot-gun" seat. It was a short drive to the wharf. I could tell we were close because the smell of the sea always smacked my nose. It was still dark but the dock lights lit up the boats and the gruff looking men that were tossing the Fish crates onto it. Each crate was filled to capacity with "moving contents." I was in awe as fish, Crustaceans, and Bivalves were loaded into a burlap bag and into a cooler of ice that I had not noticed in the bed of the pick-up. Uncle Jimmy paid the men in cash and off we went with "our" catch of the day. My Uncle Jimmy was a good cook; he always cooked for an army. But, there I was learning about Clams, Mussels, Scallops, and Shrimp. He would gut and skin the Fish with precision, removing all the bones of the Fish like a surgeon. He would remind me, "God is sacred and food is a close second." He encouraged me to never waste or play with food. Food is truly a gift from God the Father. That is something I have never forgotten to practice and pass onto all my fellow cooks.

So with a big cast iron pot let's recreate Uncle Jimmy's magic. Here is the method to his madness.

- Using Olive Oil exclusively—sauté the Carrots, Celery, Green Peppers, Leeks, Onions, and Fennel about 10 minutes on low heat.
- Dried spices accompany the vegetables along with fresh Bay Leaves (he had a Laurel tree next to his Fig tree.)
- Add fresh crushed Plum Tomatoes and a little Tomato Puree from a can.
- Simmer for about 2 hours, stirring the pot frequently.

  The Seafood was a separate preparation on its own.
- Cut the Fish into 2 inch pieces, Flour and quickly sauté in more Olive Oil. Sometimes he would add a little chopped Garlic to the pot while the Fish was cooking.
- When the Fish is golden brown, add everything else to the Fish along with 2 cups of White Wine, (actually 1 cup for the pot and 1 cup for him, he said with a chuckle.)
- After the alcohol burns off, remove the Bay Leaves from the Red Sauce and ladle the Sauce over the Seafood.
- Cover the pot to allow the Clams and Mussels to steam and open. When the lid was lifted, we all took in the wonderful aromas, gave thanks, and you guessed it . . . no one

left the table until the last bits of juices were mopped up with a piece of Bread. God bless you Uncle Jimmy for that summer of 1977.

Serves 8-10

1/2 cup	Carrot (diced)
1/2 cup	Celery (diced)
1/2 cup	Fennel (fresh, diced)
1/2 cup	Green Pepper (diced)
1/2 cup	Leeks (diced, white-part)
1/2 cup	Onion (diced)
4 T	Olive Oil
4-6 each	Plum Tomatoes (Roma-crushed)
8 oz	Tomato Puree
3-1/2 cups	*Fish Stock
4 each	Bay Leaves (laurel)
1 tsp	Oregano
1 tsp	Basil
1 tsp	Red Pepper flakes
To taste	Ground Black Pepper
To taste	Kosher Salt

SEAFOOD INGREDIENTS

1/2 lb	White fish (swordfish, sea bass, etc.)
8-10 each	Scallops (bay)
8-10 each	Shrimp (head-on)
8-10 each	Mussels (beards removed and cleaned)
8-10 each	Clams (Manila, Cherrystone, etc.)
4 T	Olive Oil
1 T	Garlic (chopped)
2 cups	White Wine
2 T	Parsley (chopped)

* Fish Stock: Recipe can be found in our "Take Stock" section on page 133.

Cantonese Mushroom Soup

While working for a Global Ministry in Colorado Springs, I was the Chef at a Conference Center that provided services for missionaries on furlough and accommodations for church groups, pastors, and, students. Our goal was to also provide work-study for many international students coming to the USA for training in the mission field. I was blessed with many students from around the globe. One student in particular was from China, the Canton region. As a way of making them feel welcomed I would ask each student to help me in creating one of the foods that was a favorite of theirs while growing up. For over a decade most of the students that worked in the kitchen contributed, in one form or another, a dish from their homeland. I'm certain that once you make and share this soup with family and friends, it will soon be a favorite for you. Without question, you will want to cook your way through each of the seven regions that make up China. By the way, when you book your travel plans be sure to call me!

- Start with sauté of Onions and Mushrooms in a stock pot with a little Sesame Oil on medium heat. Cook until the vegetables are almost dry.
- Add chopped Garlic, fresh Ginger (HHHI! GILLIGAN) and *Golden Chicken Stock.
- Bring the contents of the pot up to a slow boil.
- Season the soup to taste with all dry spices and Chicken Paste.
- Pour in Heavy Cream, Sherry Wine and Soy Sauce.
- Simmer 20 minutes.
- Thicken the soup with Cornstarch and cold stock.
- Adjust seasoning to taste if needed.
- Garnish with cooked Chicken meat, Bamboo Shoots, Snow Peas, and sliced Green Onions. Serve immediately.

Serves 6-8

I cup	White Onion (sliced)
4 cups	Mushrooms (sliced) Straw, Enoki, Shitake, Elephant Ear
I T	Sesame Oil
I qt	*Golden Chicken Stock
I qt	Heavy Cream
2-4 T	Corn Starch (mixed with equal parts of stock)
2 T	Fresh Ginger (ground)
I T	Garlic (chopped)
2 T	Chicken Paste
I/4 tsp	Cayenne Pepper
To Taste	Sherry Wine
To Taste	Soy Sauce (light)
To Taste	Ground White Pepper

GARNISH

I cup	Snow Peas (sliced)
I cup	Chicken (cooked, sliced)
I/2 cup	Bamboo Shoots (sliced)
I/2 cup	Green Onion (diced)

* Golden Chicken Stock: Recipe can be found in our "Take Stock" section on page 136.

Chicken Tortilla Soup

I'm sure, like you, I've had Tortilla Soup from Central America to Canada, all good and yet very different adaptations. Here is another one for your repertoire. This one happens to come from my neighborhood in Pueblo, Blende, as it is called, is truly a 'blend' of many cultures. The neighborhood itself is bordered by another community named Salt Creek. In Blende you will find Italians, Hispanics, and Bohemians, just to name a few. Each group brings with it a long rich history of food and celebration. And, what was cool is the fact that all cultures seem to live, work, and sometimes eat together at the local Parish during festivals or other gatherings. It was my friend, Harold, whose mother taught me how to make this recipe and several other great dishes. So, to Mrs. Archuleta I give the credit for this soup.

Follow the recipe as written or as a musician, take the notes off the page and turn them into sweet music. Add your own signature to this list of ingredients.

- Always start with a sauté of Onions and Green Chilies in a stock pot with some Oil on medium heat.
- Introduce spices and aromatics, *Golden Chicken Stock, and cook for 10 minutes.
- Add Rice and cook for 12 minutes or until rice is tender.
- Add Chicken meat and Tomatoes, cook 5 minutes more.
- Again, I like to thicken the soup slightly with Cornstarch or Arrowroot Powder.
- Season the Soup to taste.
- Ladle into bowls, garnish with Tortilla strips, Jack and Cheddar Cheese, Avocado slices, and *Crema or Sour Cream.

Serves 6-8

3-3/4 cups	*Golden Chicken Stock
1/3 cup	Long Grain Rice
1 cup	Onion (diced)
1 cup	Green Chilies (diced)
1/2 cup	Tomato (diced)
1 tsp	Cumin (ground)
1 tsp	Fresh Garlic (crushed)
1 tsp	Cilantro
2 cups	Chicken (cooked and diced)
To taste	Kosher Salt
To taste	Ground White Pepper
2-4 T	Arrowroot or Cornstarch (mixed with equal parts of stock)
2 each	Corn Tortillas (julienne and fried)

| 2 slices | Avocado (per serving) |
| Dollop | *Crema or Sour Cream |

* Golden Chicken Stock: Recipe can be found in our "Take Stock" section on page 136.

* Crema can be found in the dairy section of most food outlets.

Five Onion Soup

I know what you're thinking but, don't go there, it's not a French Onion clone. I was born on the 5th, and my favorite number is 5.

- Start with white Onions, Leeks, fresh Garlic, Red Sweet Onions, sautéed in a stock pot on medium heat in 2 tablespoons of butter.
- For the fifth (5) we will garnish with Chives. Now, whatever you do, please cook the Onions until they are brown and caramelized. This is where the flavor profile begins to deepen as the onions are cooking. The natural sugars are released and begin to brown. (Caramelize) The rule of thumb to all my fellow cooks in my kitchens over the years has been very simple . . . When baking or browning pay close attention to the color of the finished product. <u>"When its brown it's done when it's black you're done."</u>
- When the onions and leeks have wilted and caramelized, pour the Red Wine in the pot to *Deglaze, followed by some *Rich Beef Stock, Sherry Wine.
- Reduce the heat and simmer slowly for 35 to 40 minutes.
- I like to thicken the soup slightly with a little Cornstarch and *Cold Stock or Wine.
- Season the soup with Beef Paste to fortify the broth, Ground White Pepper and Salt to taste.
- Remove the soup from the stovetop and ladle into a bowl or cup.
- Float a Cheese Crouton on top, sprinkle with Chives and serve immediately.

Serves 6-8

I cup	Leeks (sliced)
I cup	White Onion (sliced)
I cup	Sweet Red Onion (sliced)
2 T	Fresh Garlic (crushed)
2 T	Fresh Chives (snipped)
2 qt	*Rich Beef Stock
I cup	Red Wine
I cup	Sherry Wine
2 T	Beef Paste
2-4 T each	Cornstarch and Cold stock mixed together
To taste	Ground White Pepper
To taste	Kosher Salt

* Rich Beef Stock: Recipe can be found in our "Take Stock" section on page 129.

* Deglaze: Using some form of alcohol or liquid to wash the bottom of the pot to recover all the browned bits of flavor.

Cheese Crouton

I each	French Baguette (I/2 inch slices cut cross-wise)
1/2 cup	Butter (melted)
1/2 cup	Parmesan Cheese (grated)

- Brush one side of baguette slices with melted Butter.
- Top with Grated Parmesan Cheese.
- Place on a baking sheet into a 350° F. oven until melted and slightly browned.
- Remove from oven and cool for use in the soup. (Be sure to make extra for your guests they will appreciate the extra pieces.)

* When possible do not use water to mix with cornstarch. Water does not provide any flavor or nutritive value, and all it really does is dilute the flavor. Use Stock, juice or spirits.

French Onion Soup Gratin

Every cookbook worth its recipes needs to have this Soup included. What makes this Soup unique is the Onions are pan roasted.

- Start with lots of Onions in a heavy bottomed roasting pot.
- Sauté dry, but stir constantly to allow the juices to flow.
- Stir in the leeks (white part only.)
- Place pot in a quick oven 450° F.
- Roast until Onions are caramelized and leeks have melted.
- Remove pot with oven mitts and return to medium heat.
- Introduce *Rich Beef Stock and bring the soup up to a slow simmer for 30-40 mins.
- At this point, add diced, seeded fresh Tomatoes and a 2 tablespoons of *Roasted Garlic Puree.
- Season the Soup with Beef Paste, Ground White Pepper, *Maggi Seasoning, Salt, and fresh grated Nutmeg.
- Simmer an additional 5 minutes, adjust seasoning as desired.
- Remove the Soup from the stovetop and ladle into oven proof bowls.
- Top with a *Toasted Garlic Crouton and 1 slice each of Gruyere and Provolone Cheeses.
- Place bowls onto a sheet tray and into to the oven at 400° F.
- Brown or *Gratin until the cheese is melted serve immediately. (Warn your guests that the Soup bowl is very hot to the touch.)

Serves 6-8

4 cup	White Onion (Julienne)
1 cup	Leek (sliced white-part only)
4 each	Green Onion (sliced)
1 T	*Roasted Garlic Puree
1 cup	Tomato (diced and seeded)
2 qt	*Rich Beef Stock
To taste	Beef Paste
To taste	Kosher Salt
To taste	Ground White Pepper
To taste	*Maggi Seasoning
To taste	Nutmeg (fresh grated)
6 each slices	Gruyere Cheese
6 each slices	Provolone Cheese

* Rich Beef Stock: Recipe can be found in our "Take Stock" section on page 129.

* Gratin: To achieve a brown or melted appearance under intense heat.

* Maggi Seasoning: Can be found in most spice sections of any food outlet.

*TOASTED GARLIC CROUTON

- Take a fresh Baguette and slice cross-wise into 1/2 inch pieces.
- Melt some Butter and add the Roasted Garlic Puree to the Butter.
- Slather one side of the Baguette and place slices on a sheet tray.
- Place in a 350° F oven and brown or toast until desired doneness.

*ROASTED GARLIC PUREE

- Place 1 cup of peeled fresh Garlic Cloves in a sauce pan.
- Add 2 cups of good Olive Oil to cover.
- Roast on top of the stove on low to medium heat until the Garlic has achieved a rich brown color. Remove from heat and allow the contents to cool before removing the Garlic.
- Reserve the Oil for your next creation.

Hungarian Bean Soup

How can I describe the sensation of taste in a hearty spoonful of flavor? The Beans, Ham, Caraway, and vegetables are ineffable. Ok let's just say there has not "Bean" a soup in my mouth I didn't love. It is tantamount for each young cook to taste as many foods as possible so that the palate can begin to recognize and distinguish between flavors and their subtleties. Incidentally, for all the young aspiring cooks out there; if you have not tasted the flavor profile of Caraway in food please take the time to find out what you have been missing. Even Zsa Zsa Gabor would give her approval to this one.

- In a stock pot sauté Carrots, Celery, Onion, Leeks and Ham shank on medium heat in zsome Butter until the vegetables are soft (4-6 minutes.)
- Pour in the *Golden Chicken Stock, soaked White Beans and Spices.
- Bring contents of the pot to a moderate boil and cook for 35-45 minutes until soft.
- Season the Soup with Beef Paste, Ground White Pepper and Salt.
- Remove Ham Shank, thicken the Soup if desired with Cornstarch and Cold Stock.
- Simmer the soup on low heat for 10 minutes.
- Adjust seasoning to taste as needed.
- Remove Soup from the stovetop and ladle into cups or bowls.
- Garnish with a dollop of Sour Cream and chopped fresh Parsley.

Serves 6-8

I cup	Carrots (diced)
I cup	Celery (diced)
I cup	Leeks (diced)
I cup	Onion (diced)
4 T	Butter
2 qt	*Golden Chicken Stock
I lb	White Beans (soaked in water in the refrigerator overnight)
2 T	Ground Caraway Seed
2 T	Hungarian Paprika
2-4 T each	Cornstarch (mixed with equal parts of Cold Stock)
To taste	Ground White Pepper
To taste	Kosher Salt
To taste	Sour Cream
2 T	Parsley (chopped)

*Golden Chicken Stock: Recipe can be found in our "Take Stock" section on page 136.

Italian Garden Soup

Another one of Nana's creations that will have you ready to Mangia! Pronto! This is a good soup for our vegan friends. Simply replace the Meat Stock with Vegetable Stock. So load it up baby with all the veggies you can handle. Did I mention this is a garden soup? There is no inconceivable way to work and live in farm country and not take advantage of the fresh produce. A large part of the rational for my career as a chef is because I worked for my Uncle Gus at his fruit and vegetable stand for three summers as a teen. Uncle Gus was a kind, soft spoken gentleman with a keen wit. He was a decorated war veteran and over the years his battle wounds would dictate the way he walked, but not his intellect and business-like mannerisms. That never stopped him from driving around in his vintage Ford pick-up to visit the local farmers, which he often did, to check on how the crops were doing. When I got my drivers license I enjoyed driving him around and listening to all the stories from a man who worked hard his entire life. My Aunt Chris was his faithful bride and she picked-up where he left off. She was a beautiful woman with a great smile and savvy business-like demeanor. I was very fond of working for and learning all I could about the business of produce from my uncle and aunt. My co-workers and I were high school friends and we worked and joked all the time during those hot summer days. We would unload literally tons of Melons, Fruits, and Vegetables on a daily basis. My friend Joe and I would tease the "big guy with the cigar" stuck in his teeth named Al. Ok the guy's name was Al, not the cigar. It was a great experience working in the fields as well. "After all, if a person wants to learn all he can about the farming business you can't sit on the front porch of the house all day and expect to learn through osmosis," said Al. So I was up at 5 a.m. and into the fields snapping Radishes as the sun was just peeking over the horizon. About 11 a.m. I was in to the washing shed to clean, weigh and bag the morning harvest, then off to the market to assist the ladies and gentlemen that drove for miles to buy from my Uncle Gus. Those are indeed cherished memories for me to recall as I write this cookbook about Soup.

- In a stock pot add the following: Carrots, Celery, Leeks, Onions, Tomatoes, and Zucchini.
- Cook veggies on medium heat in a little Olive Oil to extract all the natural juices.
- Season the pot with fresh chopped Garlic, Oregano, and Basil.
- Let the spices mingle with the vegetables for about five minutes.
- Introduce *Rich Beef Stock and let simmer for 20-30 minutes.
- Bring on the Garbanzos, Green Beans, Red Kidney Beans, and shredded Green Cabbage.
- Allow the soup to regain its simmer.
- Add protein at this point and adjust seasoning.
- Thicken if desired with Cornstarch and Cold Stock.

- Serve with a good loaf of warm Bread.

Serves 6-8

I cup	Carrots (diced)
I cup	Celery (diced)
I cup	Leeks (sliced)
I cup	Onion (diced)
I cup	Tomatoes (diced)
I cup	Zucchini (diced)
2 qt	*Rich Beef Stock or *Vegetable Stock
4 T	Olive Oil
2 T	Garlic (chopped)
2 T	Oregano Leaves
2 T	Basil Leaves
I cup	Garbanzo Beans
I cup	Kidney Beans
I cup	Green Beans
I cup	Green Cabbage (shredded)
½ lb	Meat of choice (cooked and diced)
To taste	Ground White Pepper
To taste	Kosher Salt
2-4 T each	Cornstarch and Cold stock mixed together

* Rich Beef Stock: Recipe can be found in our "Take Stock" section on page 129.

* Vegetable Stock: Recipe can be found in our "Take Stock" section on page 132.

Indian Summer Soup

This is a wonderful contribution from our Native American cooks. A number of honored guests can step up and be the star of this Chef's soup pot. Be it Hubbard, Butternut, Acorn, to name a few. Hey! Did you know that the word "Chef" is actually derived from the Indian word for Chief? Ya Ta Hay! As each of us begins to climb the ladder to achieve the title as Chef one day, remember, the basic building blocks of the cooking process. Master those basics through consistent practice and execution each day in the kitchen. Each step in the cooking process and development of a dish is intended to build flavor, texture, shape and appearance. The dish needs to look, smell, and above all else, taste good. Some of the shortfalls that plague young cooks are that they fail to cook the individual ingredients before combining the other flavorings. In other words, every time we use water for a soup we are truly discrediting the true flavor of the other ingredients. The water dilutes the flavors and in some instances, it cuts short the flavor profile. Another shortfall we see comes from the television competitive cooking shows everyday—that is the lack of proper seasoning practices. This cannot happen unless the cook forgets or just decides to not taste his or her product as it goes through the stages of the cooking and finishing process. Please! Please! Please! Taste the food as it flows through the steps of completion.

- In a stock pot, sauté some Onions in butter on medium heat until caramelized.
- Add the Squash, which has been roasted in the oven.
- Cook on medium heat for 10 minutes stirring as needed.
- Introduce the Cilantro and the Cumin, *Golden Chicken Stock.
- Cook an additional 10-15 minutes.
- Remove from heat and puree using a food mill or immersion blender wand.
- Place pureed Soup back into pot, add Heavy Cream and bring Soup back to simmer.
- Season the Soup to taste with Ground White Pepper and Salt.
- Remove the soup from the stovetop and garnish with fresh chopped Cilantro.
- Ladle the Soup into cups or bowls and serve.

❖ A fun idea for serving your guests is to purchase Baby Pumpkins which have been seeded and steamed enough to soften the cavity, but able to retain it's shape. Fill the Pumpkins with Soup and replace crown.

Serves 6-8

1 cup	White Onion (sliced)
3 cups	Squash (peeled, seeded, diced and roasted)
2 tsp	Cilantro
2 tsp	Cumin
2 qt	*Golden Chicken Stock

2 cups	Heavy Cream
2 T each	Cornstarch and Cold stock mixed together
2 T	Butter
To Taste	Kosher Salt
To Taste	Ground White Pepper

* Golden Chicken Stock: Recipe can be found in our "Take Stock" section on page 136.

Roasted Squash

- Toss peeled, diced and seeded squash in a little Olive Oil to coat.
- Place on a sheet tray in a 350° F oven for 35-45 minutes until the Squash is softened and golden brown.
- Remove from oven and place in the stock pot along with the Onions.

Roasted Tomatillo and Chicken Soup

Ask me what my favorite salsa is . . . something with fresh Tomatillos in it. This is not a glorified Chicken Tortilla Soup, the flavor of the Tomatillo stands by itself boldly along side the Green Chilies and aromatics. The Tomatillo is a unique fruit that is grown throughout the western hemisphere. I spent time with a family in Guatemala that grew the fabled fruit and sold it daily in the market outside their casita. Make no mistake this is not green un-ripened domestic Tomato. These husk tomatoes are truly in a category by themselves. Give this recipe a try and I'm sure you will find many uses for this versatile Love Apple.

- In a stock pot, sauté Onions, Garlic and roasted Tomatillos in Olive Oil on medium heat.
- Cook for 10 to 15 minutes until the Onions are soft.
- Introduce *Golden Chicken Stock, Cumin, Mexican Oregano, and Red Chili Powder.
- Bring the contents of the pot to a slow boil.
- Reduce the heat to a simmer.
- Simmer for 20-30 minutes until the Tomatillos are softened.
- Season soup with Chicken Paste, Ground White Pepper and Salt.
- Thicken with Arrowroot Powder and Cold Stock if desired.
- Remove the Soup from the stovetop.
- Place cooked Rice, cooked Chicken meat, and chopped fresh Cilantro in a cup or bowl and pour the hot soup over the top of ingredients.
- Serve immediately.

Serves 6-8

I cup	Onions (sliced)
2 T	Garlic (chopped)
2 lb	Tomatillos (peeled, roasted, chopped)
2 qt	*Golden Chicken Stock
2 T	Ground Cumin
I T	Mexican Oregano
I T	Red Chili Powder
2 T	Chicken Paste
To taste	Ground White Pepper
To taste	Kosher Salt
2-4 T each	Arrowroot Powder and Cold stock mixed together

* Golden Chicken Stock: Recipe can be found in our "Take Stock" section on page 136.

Roasted Tomatillos

- Place husked, halved tomatillos on a baking sheet.
- Drizzle Olive Oil to cover and roast in a 350° F oven for 35-40 minutes until the Tomatillos begin to blister and brown.
- Remove from the oven and cool prior to use in the soup.

GARNISH

I lb	Chicken meat (cooked, diced)
1/2 lb	Brown Rice (cooked)
2 T	Cilantro (chopped)

Sicilian Spinach Soup

This Soup was and is still a family favorite around the dinner table. Walking through my Nana's kitchen, I could always tell when this Soup was being created. Sautéed Onions, fresh Spinach from the fields, fresh Basil from the herb garden transported me back to a time when life as a 13-year-old growing up on the farm was full of new and exciting adventures. Then I could smell the flavor-packed broth from the pot where the bird of sacrifice was stewing; which brought together all the components for this great family Soup with Sicilian flair. I'm not quite sure how she did it, but it was always a dash or splash of this, that, and the other. Laced with some fresh crushed Garlic, dried Oregano, and Chicken Paste to fortify the soup, forty minutes later it was time to find my chair at the table. The Soup always had some Pasta in it. As the Soup continued to simmer on the stove the Pasta would swell and the soup got thicker which displaced much of the broth.

- In a stock pot sauté Onions and Garlic along with Oregano.
- Introduce *Golden Chicken Stock.
- Season broth with Chicken Paste, Ground White Pepper, and Kosher Salt.
- Cook for 15-20 minutes to develop the flavors.
- Add the fresh Spinach and Basil.
- Cook an additional 5 minutes.
- Finish with a splash of fresh squeezed Lemon Juice and some grated Romano Cheese.
- Place a fair amount of Pasta and cooked Chicken meat in a bowl and ladle the broth over the top.

Serves 6-8

1 cup	Onion (sliced)
1 lb	Fresh Spinach (de-stemmed)
2 T	Fresh Basil Leaves (chopped)
2 T	Garlic (crushed)
2 T	Oregano (dried)
2 qt	*Golden Chicken Stock
2 T	Chicken Paste
1 lb	Chicken meat (cooked, shredded)
To taste	Ground White Pepper
To taste	Kosher Salt
1 lb	Pasta (cooked)
1/2 cup	Romano Cheese (grated)
To taste	Lemon (fresh squeezed)

* Golden Chicken Stock: Recipe can be found in our "Take Stock" section on page 136.

Sopa de Guatemala

I had the great honor and privilege of drilling for water in the Mayan Highlands of Guatemala. My love for the people is equal to the passion I have for the cuisine. Each day at lunch we were served a Soup of vegetables and "some kind of meat." It was slightly seasoned, having a very nourishing appeal to it. The flavors were reminiscent of the region; earthy, clean, with overtones of Chili and other indigenous spices. Usually the soup was accompanied by White Corn Tamales as a substitute for Bread or even Tortillas. The protein or "some kind of meat" as we called it, was Beef or Chicken on the bone. My fellow laborers would ask me, 'from what part of the Chicken did this piece come," as they waved it in my face. I'd simply reply, "The edible part." I was able to observe the ladies of the village as they prepared the Soup to be served to us. I have added some "touches" to this basic recipe that reminded me of the agricultural bounty that is grown in their country. It could very well be a meal once you're done creating.

- Begin with a stock pot filled with 2 quarts of *Golden Chicken Stock.
- Season the stock with Chicken Paste to fortify the soup, Cumin, *Epazote, crushed Garlic, Ground White Pepper.
- Add the vegetables to the seasoned broth and bring the contents of the pot up to a *Slow boil.
- Reduce heat and allow the Soup to develop the flavors (30-40 minutes.)
- Add cooked meat of your choice, cooked Beans, and Tomato Juice.
- Bring the Soup back up to a boil and cook an additional 10 minutes.
- Thicken the soup with Cornstarch and Cold Stock.
- Continue cooking for 5 minutes more.
- Adjust seasonings as needed.
- Remove the Soup from the stovetop.
- Ladle into cups or bowls.
- Serve with Warm White Corn Tortillas.

Serves 6-8

1 cup	Carrots (sliced)
1 cup	Celery (sliced)
1 cup	Onions (sliced)
1 cup	Green Chilies (chopped)
1 cup	Squash (sliced) Calabasita, Crook neck, and Zucchini
2 qt	*Golden Chicken Stock
2 cups	Tomato Juice
2 T	Garlic (crushed)
2 T	Cumin

2 T	*Epazote
1 lb	Chicken (cooked, diced)
1/2 lb	Red Kidney or Pinto Beans (cooked)
To taste	Chicken Paste
To taste	Ground White Pepper
To taste	Kosher Salt
2-4 T each	Cornstarch and Cold Stock mixed together

* Golden Chicken Stock: Recipe can be found in our "Take Stock" section on page 136.

*Epazote: Mexican herb resembles Oregano but is much stronger in flavor, use sparingly.

*Slow boil: Culinary term for tiny bubbles just breaking the surface of the pot.

Swedish Onion Soup

A good "comfort soup" to eat on those cold winter months or rainy days. The flavor of roasted Onions, Potatoes, and Nutmeg in a beefy creamy blanket of broth will no doubt sharpen the senses and warm the soul. Serve with Cheese Toast and a green salad. The only thing missing is a glass of your favorite Wine and your soul mate to share it with.

- Start this recipe by roasting julienne Onions in a pan with some butter at 400°F.
- Stir every 5 minutes until brown (35-40 minutes.)
- Transfer the browned Onions to stock pot and pour in *Rich Beef Stock.
- Bring the pot up to a moderate boil.
- Reduce the heat and simmer 20-30 minutes.
- Add diced Potatoes and cook until potatoes are tender—about 10 more minutes.
- Pour Heavy Cream down the sides of the pot to minimize *Temperature plunge.
- Bring the soup back to a boil and cook 5 minutes more.
- Season the Soup with Beef Paste, Ground White Pepper, Nutmeg and Salt.
- Thicken with cornstarch and Cold stock if desired.
- Adjust seasonings to taste.
- Serve with warm Cheese Toast.

Serves 6-8

4 cups	Onions (sliced)
2 cups	Potatoes (peeled and diced)
4 T	Butter
2 qt	*Rich Beef Stock
2 cups	Heavy Cream
To taste	Beef Paste
To taste	Ground White Pepper
To taste	Nutmeg (fresh grated)
To taste	Kosher Salt

* Rich Beef Stock: Recipe can be found in our "Take Stock" section on page 129.

* Temperature plunge: Occurs when a cold liquid is introduced into a hot liquid slowing down the cooking process.

Cheese Toast

- Brush one side of baguette slices with melted Butter and garlic.
- Top with grated Parmesan Cheese.
- Place on a baking sheet into a 350° F oven until melted and slightly browned. Remove from oven and cool for use in the soup. (Be sure to make extra for your guests. They will appreciate the extra pieces.)

I each	French Baguette (1/2 inch slices cut cross-wise)
1/2 cup	Butter (melted)
I T	Garlic (minced)
I cup	Parmesan Cheese (grated)

Swiss Onion Soup

There is certainly nothing neutral about this bowl of hearty goodness. With lots of Leeks and Onions to start the cascade of flavors, brace yourself. I love this Soup when I'm sitting on the ice trying to entice a big Brown or Rainbow Trout or for that matter anywhere in the great outdoors of Colorado. The Soup travels quite well in a thermos bottle. When entertaining guests at home, I like to serve this Soup with Parmesan Cheese twists.

- In a stock pot sauté the Onions in Butter over medium high heat until brown and caramelized.
- Add the Leeks and cook for 5-6 minutes.
- Introduce a good White Wine and braise until Leeks are soft (4-6 minutes.)
- Pour in *Rich Brown Stock and Tomato Juice.
- Bring the contents of the pot to a slow boil for 15-20 minutes.
- Season the Soup with Beef Paste to fortify the Soup, Ground White Pepper and Salt.
- Thicken if desired with White Wine and Cornstarch. (Remember it's that mouth feel thing for me.)
- Adjust seasoning if needed and remove the Soup from the stovetop.
- Ladle the soup into cups or bowls.

Serves 6-8

2 cups	Leeks (sliced)
2 cups	Onions (sliced)
4 T	Butter
2 qt	*Rich Beef Stock
I cup	White Wine
I cup	Tomato Juice
2 T	Beef Paste
2 T	Ground White Pepper
2 T	Kosher Salt
2-4 T each	Cornstarch and White Wine mixed together

* Rich Beef Stock: Recipe can be found in our "Take Stock" section on page 129.

Parmesan Cheese Twists

I like to use Pizza dough for this recipe.

- Just take your favorite dough rolled out on a cutting board or counter top.
- Using a fork pierce the dough randomly, but evenly on one side.
- Brush with a good extra Virgin Olive Oil.
- Sprinkle dried Basil, Oregano, and Red Pepper flakes—Yikes! Not too many.
- Follow with a generous amount of grated Parmesan Cheese.
- Fold dough over like closing a book.
- Take a knife or Pizza cutter and cut 1/2 inch strips of dough.
- Using your fingers pick up 1 piece with each end tightly grasped, twist in opposite directions until desired shape is achieved.
- Place on greased or paper-lined sheet tray.
- Bake in a hot oven at 400° F until golden brown.

TAKE STOCK

Rich Beef Stock

- In a roasting pan place the Veal bones which have been thoroughly washed and rinsed.
- Roast the bones until they are brown in a 400° F oven.
- Add the *Mirepoix and continue roasting until the Onions begin to caramelize.
- Remove the pan from the oven to stovetop.
- Place the contents of the pan into a stock pot.
- Turn the heat low to warm up the caramelized residue on the bottom of the pan.
- *Deglaze with the Red Wine scraping the residue or browned bits off the bottom of the pan and pour this into the stock pot.
- Fill the pot 2/3 full of cold water and toss in the *Sachet bag.
- Bring the contents of the pot up to a moderate boil.
- Remove any impurities with a skimmer or ladle.
- Reduce the heat to a simmer and allow the stock to develop for 4-6 hours.
- Remove the *Sachet bag and strain the stock through a *Rinsed cheesecloth-lined china cap or wire mesh strainer.
- Discard the bones and remnants in the pot.
- Cool and refrigerate the stock until needed. The stock can be frozen for no longer than 3 months.

Yield 1 gallon.

2 gal.	Filtered Water
5 lb.	Veal bones
2 c	Red Wine

* Mirepoix: Rough cut Carrots, Celery, Leeks, Onions and Mushroom pieces (not stems.)

* Sachet bag: Bay Leaves, Black Peppercorns (crushed) Parsley stems and Thyme.

* Rinsed Cheesecloth: Take the cheesecloth out of the package it came in and rinse in cold water to remove any sizing material that may have been used in its production. The cold water will also tighten up the holes for better straining.

Oxtail Stock

The Rich Beef Stock recipe can be used for the Oxtail Stock.

- Cut the pieces of Oxtail about 1 inch long. (Beef Marrow bones can also be used if Oxtail is not available.)

Lamb Stock

The Rich Beef Stock recipe can be used for the Lamb Stock.

- Reduce the simmer time on the Lamb stock to 2 hours maximum.
- Roast the Marrow bones as you would use the Beef Stock recipe method.

Vegetable Stock

- Fill the pot 3/4 full of cold water and toss in the Vegetables and *Sachet bag.
- Bring the contents of the pot up to a *Slow boil and then reduce heat to a simmer for 1 hour.
- Remove the *Sachet bag and strain the stock through a *Rinsed cheesecloth-lined china cap or wire mesh strainer.
- Discard the remnants in the pot.
- Cool and refrigerate the stock until needed.

The stock can be frozen for no longer than 3 months.
Yield 2 gal.

2 gal	Filtered Water
1/4 lb. each	Vegetables: Carrots, Celery, Fennel, Leeks, Mushrooms, Tomatoes and Parsley (rough-cut.)

* Sachet bag: Bay Leaves, Black Peppercorns (crushed) and Thyme.

* Rinsed Cheesecloth: Take the cheesecloth out of the package it came in and rinse in cold water to remove any sizing material that may have been used in its production. The cold water will also tighten up the holes for better straining.

* Slow-boil: Culinary term for small bubbles just breaking the surface of the pot.

Fish Stock

- In a stock pot place Fish scraps and bones, *Mirepoix, Wine and *Sachet bag.
- Pour cold water over the contents of the pot to fill 3/4 full of capacity.
- Bring this up to a slow boil reduce the heat and simmer for 40 minutes.
- Skim any impurities that may boil up to the surface.
- Strain through a *Rinsed Cheesecloth-lined china cap or wire mesh strainer.
- Cool and refrigerate until needed.

Fish Stock can be frozen for no longer than 2 months.

Yield 1-1/2 gallon.

2 gal.	Filtered Water
5 lb.	White Fish Bones (Halibut, Bass e.g.)
2 c	White Wine

* Mirepoix: Rough cut Celery, Onions, and Leeks.

* Sachet bag: Bay Leaves, Black Peppercorns (crushed) Coriander, Parsley, and Thyme.

* Rinsed Cheesecloth: take the cheesecloth out of the package it came in and rinse in cold water to remove any sizing material that may have been used in its production. The cold water will also tighten up the holes for better straining.

Lobster Stock

- Place the shells, legs and claws of the Lobster and *Sachet bag in a stock pot.
- Pour cold water over the contents of the pot to fill 3/4 of the capacity.
- Bring this up to a slow boil and then reduce the heat to a simmer for 30 minutes.
- Strain through a *Rinsed Cheesecloth-lined china cap or wire mesh strainer.
- Cool and refrigerate until needed.

Lobster stock can be frozen for no longer than 2 months.
Yield 1 gal.

1-1/2 gal.   Filtered Water
Lobster shells, legs and claws equal to 2 whole Lobsters.

* Sachet bag: Bay Leaves, Coriander, Rosemary and Dill

* Rinsed Cheesecloth: Take the cheesecloth out of the package it came in and rinse in cold water to remove any sizing material that may have been used in its production. The cold water will also tighten up the holes for better straining.

Salmon Stock

- In a stock pot place Salmon scraps and bones, *Mirepoix and *Sachet bag.
- Pour cold water over the contents of the pot to fill 3/4 full of capacity.
- Bring this up to a slow boil and then reduce the heat and simmer for 40 minutes.
- Skim any impurities that may boil up to the surface.
- Strain through a *Rinsed cheesecloth-lined china cap or wire mesh strainer.
- Cool and refrigerate until needed.

Fish Stock can be frozen for no longer than 2 months.

Yield 1-1/2 gallon.

2 gal	Filtered Water
4 lbs.	Salmon bones and scraps (2/3 Bones to 1/3 Skin)

* Mirepoix: Rough cut Celery, Leeks and Onions (1/4 lb each.) French term for vegetables used to fortify a stock.

* Sachet bag: Bay Leaves, Coriander, Rosemary and Dill.

* Rinsed Cheesecloth: Take the cheesecloth out of the package it came in and rinse in cold water to remove any sizing material that may have been used in its production. The cold water will also tighten up the holes for better straining.

Golden Chicken Stock

- In a roasting pan place Chicken bones which have been thoroughly washed and rinsed.
- Roast the bones until they are brown in a 400° F oven.
- Add the *Mirepoix and continue roasting until the Onions begin to caramelize.
- Remove the pan from the oven and place on stovetop.
- Place the contents into a stock pot.
- Turn the heat to low to warm up the caramelized residue on the bottom of the pan.
- *Deglaze with the White Wine scraping the residue or browned bits off the bottom of the pan and pour this into the stock pot.
- Fill the pot 3/4 full of cold water and toss in the *Sachet bag.
- Bring the contents of the pot up to a moderate boil.
- Removing any impurities with a skimmer or ladle.
- Reduce the heat to a simmer and allow the stock to develop for 4-6 hours.
- Remove the *Sachet bag and strain the stock through a *Rinsed cheesecloth-lined china cap or wire mesh strainer.
- Discard the bones and remnants in the pot.
- Cool, refrigerate the stock until needed.

The stock can be frozen for no longer than 3 months.
Yield 1 gal.

2 gal	Filtered Water
4 lb.	Raw Chicken bones (necks, backs, wings) and *Cocks' comb when available.
1 c	White wine

* Mirepoix: Rough-cut Carrots, Celery, Leeks and Onions (1/4 lb each.)

* Sachet Bag: Bay Leaves, Black Peppercorns (crushed) Parsley stems, Rosemary, and Thyme.

*Rinsed Cheesecloth: Make sure to wash the cheesecloth in cold water to remove any sizing material that may have been used in the processing of the cloth. The water will also shrink the holes in the cheesecloth for better straining.

*Cocks' comb has become a prized part of the Chicken for its' gelatinous qualities which enhance and fortify good stocks.

Pheasant Stock

The *Golden Chicken Stock recipe can be used to make the Pheasant Stock but be sure to include the legs of the Pheasant along with the rest of the carcass except the breast. The legs contain more cartilage and tendons than usable meat.

Duck Stock

The *Golden Chicken Stock recipe can be used to make the Duck Stock. Simply substitute the Duck carcass and legs. (Make sure to roast the bones to deepen the flavor profile.) The Duck breast is to be roasted and diced for the garnish.

Cooking Terms and Measurements

Bisque: A thick cream soup.

Blanch: To immerse in rapidly boiling water and allow cooking slightly.

Bloom: To heat or toast an herb or spice to release its flavors.

Butter-poach: To gently cook a food in 2/3 Butter to 1/3 stock or water.

Brunoise: Very small dice of vegetables and meat for a sauce or soup.

Caramelize: To heat a raw food in order to release the sugars which in turn will brown and add flavor to a dish.

Chiffonade: Very fine julienne of meat or vegetables used as a final garnish.

Clarified Butter: Butter that has been simmered slowly to remove all the milk solids.

Consommé: Protein or vegetable stock that has been intensely flavored by a process of extraction.

Crème Fraiche: French term for thick unsweetened dairy cream.

Deglaze: To wash the bottom of a pot with a liquid to loosen and remove caramelized bits of protein or vegetable residue using alcohol, juice or stock.

Dredge: To coat lightly with flour, cornmeal, etc.

Gratin: Topped with cheese and browned in oven or under broiler.

Holy Trinity: Cajun term for celery, green pepper and carrots.

Infused: To let food stand in hot liquid in order to extract or enhance the flavor.

Julienne: To cut or slice vegetables or meat in matchstick size pieces.

Marinate: To allow a food to stand in a liquid in order to tenderize or to add flavor.

Mince: To chop food into very small pieces.

Mirepoix: French term for carrots, celery, and onion for use in a stock or soup.

Mouth-feel: Smooth-texture-like feeling of food on the tongue and palate.

Parboil: To boil until partially cooked.

Poach: To cook gently in hot liquid kept just below the boiling point.

Puree: To mash or blend food in a food processor until velvety smooth.

Raft: Mixture of egg whites, ground meat and vegetables used in consommé production.

Roast: To cook in an oven until the food has become browned and concentrated in flavor.

Roux: Equal amounts of melted butter or fat and flour cooked to form a thickening agent for soups and stocks.

Sachet bag: Spices and herbs tied up in a piece of cheesecloth and placed in a stock pot of liquid to enhance flavor.

Sauté: To cook and/or brown food in a small quantity of hot fat.

Simmer: To cook food just below the boiling point.

Shock: To plunge a food that has been partially cooked in an ice-bath.

Slow-Boil: Culinary term for small bubbles just breaking the surface of a pot of liquid.

Stock: Mixture of vegetables and/or meat simmered in water to build a base for sauces and soups.

Temperature plunge: Pouring a cold liquid into a hot liquid slowing or stopping the cooking process.

Toss: To combine ingredients using a repeated lifting motion.

Veloute: Thickened stock with the addition of cream.

Viscosity: Thickness of a soup or sauce.

MEASUREMENTS   EQUIVALENTS

A pinch	1/8 teaspoon or less	Dash	<	1/8 teaspoon
3 teaspoons	1 tablespoon	1 T	=	3 teaspoons
4 tablespoons	1/4 cup	4 T	=	1/4 cup
8 tablespoons	1/2 cup	5-1/2 T	=	1/3 cup
12 tablespoons	3/4 cup	8 T	=	1/2 cup
16 tablespoons	1 cup	10 2/3 T	=	2/3 cup
2 cups	1 pint	12 T	=	3/4 cup
4 cups	2 quarts	16 T	=	1 cup
4 quarts	1 gallon	1 cup	=	8 fluid oz.
8 quarts	1 peck	1 cup	=	1 pint
4 pecks	1 bushel	2 cups	=	1 pint
16 ounces	1 pound	4 cups	=	1 quart
32 ounces	1 quart	2 pints	=	1 quart
1 ounce liquid	2 tablespoons	4 quarts	=	1 gallon
8 ounces liquid	1 cup	12 oz can	=	1-1/2 cups
		16 oz can	=	2 cups
Use standard measuring spoons and		20 oz can	=	2-1/2 cups
cup. All measurements are level.		28.5 oz can	=	3-1/2 cups
		56 oz can	=	7 cups

C° TO F° CONVERSION

120° C	250°F
140° C	275°F
150° C	300°F
160° C	325°F
180° C	350° F
190° C	375° F
200° C	400° F
220° C	425° F
230° C	450° F

Temperature conversions are estimates.

Herbs, Spices, and Aromatics

Dried vs. Fresh. While dried herbs are convenient, they don't generally have the same purity of flavor as fresh herbs. Check the freshness of dried herbs for bright colors not dull faded shades. Crush a few leaves in between your fingers to see if the aroma is still strong. Always store dried herbs away from direct sunlight and heat. Herbs should be stored in an air-tight container.

Allspice: Strong, sweet flavor. Good in Caribbean dishes, soups, desserts.

Arrowroot Powder: No flavor, used as a thickening agent for soups, stew, gravies. Not as strong as cornstarch.

Basil Leaves: Sweet, warm flavor with an aromatic odor. Use whole or ground. Good with lamb, fish, roast, stews, beef, vegetables, dressings and omelets.

Bay Leaves: Pungent flavor. Use whole leaf but remove before serving. Good in vegetable dishes, seafood, stews, and pickles.

Black Pepper: The Master spice. Strong, hot, sharp. Good in all foods.

Caraway: Spicy taste and aromatic smell. Use in cake, breads, soups, cheeses, and sauerkraut.

Cayenne Pepper: Hot, intense, spicy. Where heat is needed this is the spice to use.

Chervil: Distinctive, warm, hint of menthol. Known as Gourmet's parsley.

Chives: Sweet, mild flavor like that of onion. Excellent in salads, fish, soups, and potatoes.

Cilantro: Green plant of the coriander seed. Use in fish, chicken, rice, soups. Chinese parsley.

Cinnamon: Sweet, pungent flavor. Widely used in baked goods, chocolate dishes, chutneys, and hot drinks.

Cloves: Very powerful, warm, sweet. Use in soups, stews, baked goods, desserts.

Cornstarch: Corn-based thickening agent used in soups, stews, sauces, gravies and dessert making.

Coriander: Mild, sweet, orange flavor. Common in curry dishes, chutney, pickling spice.

Cumin: Slightly bitter, warm, powerful taste. Good in curries, chili, soups, and Mexican cuisine.

Curry Powder: Spices are combined to proper proportions to give a distinct flavor.

Dill: Both seeds and leaves are flavorful. Cook with fish, soups, dressings, potatoes and pickles.

Epazote: Similar to oregano. Strong flavor. Good in Mexican dishes.

Fennel: Anise flavor, pairs well with Mediterranean dishes, seafood dishes.

Garlic: Onion family, strong, intense, and hot.

Garlic Powder: Dehydrated garlic ground into a powder.

Ginger: A pungent root, this aromatic spice is sold fresh, dried or ground. Use in Asian and Pan Pacific Cuisines.

Gumbo File: Ground Sassafras leaves. Used mainly in Cajun and Creole style cooking.

Honey Powder: Dehydrated and ground into a powder. Used as a sweetener in place of sugar.

Kosher Salt: Salt which contains no iodine and has a larger crystal.

Mace: Outer shell of the nutmeg. Good for soups and stocks.

Marjoram: Both dried and fresh available. Use in fish, poultry, tomato dishes, lamb, stews.

Mexican Oregano: Stronger than the American variety. Use in all Mexican and Latin dishes.

Mint: Aromatic with a cool flavor. Great in beverages, fish, lamb, soups, vegetables, and fruit dishes.

Nutmeg: Whole or ground. Used in cream soups, chicken dishes, veal, cakes, and pies.

Onion Powder: Dehydrated onion that has been ground into a powder form.

Oregano: Strong, aromatic odor. Use whole or ground in tomato products, fish, pizza, poultry, stews, and vegetables.

Spanish paprika: A bright red pepper. Slightly hot flavor used in meat dishes, soups, vegetables, salads, and potatoes.

Parsley: Best when used fresh. Good in garnishing, use with fish, soups, meat, and potatoes.

Red Pepper Flakes: Dried, hot red peppers that have been crushed. Excellent where a little heat is desired.

Rosemary: Very aromatic. Can be used fresh or dried. Season beef, pork, seafood, soups, bread, potatoes, and dressings.

Sea Salt: Salt crystals harvested using sea water. Good in all seafood and fish dishes.

Shallots: Onion-like flavor with garlicky overtones. Good in soups, sauces, meat dishes, marinades, and breads.

Thyme: Aromatic flavor. Great with lamb, pork, veal, and poultry. Good grilling spice or use in marinades.

White Pepper: Slightly milder and sweeter than black pepper.

Flavorings and Enhancements

Beef Paste: Roasted beef flavoring used to fortify a soup or sauce.

Chicken Paste: Roasted chicken flavoring used to fortify a soup or sauce.

Clam Paste: Cooked clam flavoring used to fortify a soup or sauce.

Ham Paste: Roasted cured ham flavoring used to fortify a soup or sauce.

Hot Pepper Sauce: Red peppers, vinegar and salt. Used to add hot, sharp flavor to foods.

Lea and Perrins Sauce: Peppery, piquant similar to Worcestershire.

Liquid Smoke: Concentrated hickory flavored wood sugars.

Maggi Seasoning: Beefy flavored, peppery sauce for seasoning soups.

Soy Sauce: Fermented soy bean based sauce used in Asian and Pan-Pacific cuisine.

References

Inner Harbor—Baltimore, Maryland
USS. Constellation—United States Navy
St. Charles Mesa—Pueblo, Colorado
Martha's Vineyard—Connecticut
LaJolla Beach—LaJolla, California
Kissing Camels Golf Club—Sunrise Management Co.
Pueblo Country Club—Pueblo, Colorado
C. F. & I Steel Mill—Pueblo, Colorado
San Diego—California Tourism Board
Manhattan—New York Tourism Bureau
Lake Okoboji—Iowa State Parks Commission
Brookings—Kansas Board of Tourism
Kansas Division of Wildlife
New Orleans—Louisiana Board of Tourism
Daniel Webster—Webster's Dictionary
Punxatawny Phil—Pennsylvania Board of Tourism
Sailor-man, Bluto, and Olive Oyle—Courtesy of Looney Tunes.
Grand Marais Minnesota Board of Tourism
Owjibwa and Chippewa—First Nations People.
Minsk and Volga—Union of Democratic States (USSR)
San Francisco California Tourism Board
Canton—China Board of Tourism
Gilligan—Courtesy of Screen Gems Films
Salt Creek—Pueblo, Colorado
Harold Archuleta—Pueblo, Colorado
Zsa Zsa Gabor
Grace Giadone—used by permission
Chris and Gus Giadone—Pueblo, Colorado
Guatemala and Mayan Highlands Board of Tourism
Blende, Colorado
William Wallace—Scotland Board of Tourism
Shawnee Park—Parks Department of Iowa
Capitol—Washington D.C.
Andalusia—Spain Departmento de Tourismo
Kathmandu and Madras—India Board of Tourism
Denver Colorado Board of Tourism
Ken and Sandy—Colorado Springs, Colorado
Willy Wonka—Courtesy of Warner Brothers Inc.